Successful

Sales Management

Mark Johns

SUCCESSFUL SALES MANAGEMENT

By Mark Johns
© 2011 Mark Johns

ISBN 978-0-9835376-0-1

Success Press International
3818 Far West Boulevard, #105
Austin, TX 78731
(512) 795-2931
www.markjohnsbooks.com
www.markjohns-ebooks.com

CONTENTS

Why Read This Book?

"Perhaps this book's greatest message is stated on the back cover: *No one was born a great sales manager. Those who are successful learned to be. They got the education they needed, they learned and practiced the skills of managing salespeople and they improved by doing it. You can, too.* Read the book and keep it handy."
– **Don F. Lowe**, CEO, Franchise Services, Inc.

"The most successful business owners and executives on the planet know something other people don't. And that is, the toughest, most important job in any company is the job of the sales manager. Great sales managers propel the success of an enterprise while average sales managers slowly choke the life out of even the most robust of opportunities. Mark Johns knows what it takes to be a great sales manager. He knows, because he's studied sales management for decades AND because he's a great sales manager himself. In *Successful Sales Management*, he lays out exactly what a sales manager needs to do - and he lays it out in practical, actionable steps that you can start today. If you have something to sell - you'll profit handsomely from this fine book."
– **Jack Hayhow**, CEO, Opus, www.opuskc.com

"Stick to the basics and you'll never have to go back to them! With Mark Johns' new book he covers the key fundamentals that will help you recruit, train and motivate your team to greater success."
– **Barry Farber**, www.BarryFarber.com

"I've had the good fortune to work alongside Mark Johns for more than a dozen years and I love his approach to sales and sales management. Whether he is working with a novice salesperson or an experienced salesperson, he is able to relate and impart insight that the salesperson is able to quickly apply and see better results. It's this realistic approach to his coaching that makes him so sought after from sales people and business owners alike. If you have the chance to read his book – do it. If you have the chance to work alongside him – do it. You and your business will benefit from both!"

> – **Chuck Lennon**, President, TeamLogicIT, www.TeamLogicIT.com

"If you are responsible for sales management, this book is a must read. As a new sales manager, I have gained the knowledge and confidence necessary to succeed by implementing the strategies Mark so clearly presents. From the first page to the last, this book will provide invaluable insight over a wide range of components essential for your success. If you are serious about your career, read this book – you'll send Mark a thank you card after you do."

> – **Richard Coriaty**, 5 Time National Salesperson of the Year Award Recipient, Sir Speedy Printing

"Most books about how to sell leave out of the equation the person who directs the sales staff. Mark Johns adroitly, specifically, directly and with stories and anecdotes galore addresses the all-important issue of how to hire, train and motivate your sales staff. If you can book him, I'd do it for my next sales meeting!"

> – **Jerry Hanson**, Professional Speaker, Sales Trainer and Llama Packer

"This is just what every business owner or sales manager needs as they decide to move their business forward through a sales team. Mark has laid out straightforward strategies, which are easy to follow. Even better, the actionable tactics are easy to apply. For more than 15 years, I have been coaching business owners and entrepreneurs who are growing their business from the ground up, and I strongly recommend this as a must read, must implement as they hire their sales people. My clients will. "

> – **Coach Paul Currie**, actionCOACH of Central Pennsylvania, *North America's #1 Business Coaching Firm*

"Mark nailed it! For any producers or those managing producers, Mark provides you the textbook of how to - from recruiting, hiring, training, managing and coaching he covers it all in a structured, practical and easy-to-incorporate approach. Far more than just another book on sales management, this is truly a hands-on field guide for those of us looking to effectively lead successful producers!"

> – **Mike Greene**, Integrity Works Coaching www.integrityworkscoaching.com

Most "big" businesses have professional sales managers. Most small business owners have to learn to be effective at recruiting, hiring, training, managing and coaching salespeople. Mark Johns has written the playbook, covering each of those challenges in depth. Reading this book with dramatically increase your chances of success!

> – **Dave Fellman**, author of *Listen To The Dinosaur (The Fundamentals of Selling Haven't Changed!)* www.DaveFellman.com

Preface

Most likely, you are a reluctant sales manager. You own a business, you have one or more sales representatives and someone has to manage them. Lucky you.

Or, maybe you've decided you need one or more sales representatives and you'll have to manage them – after you recruit, hire and train them. Lucky you.

My hope is that once you get into these pages, you'll be thinking, "Lucky me. This is just what I need!"

That's why I wrote this book. For more than fifteen years, I've been speaking, teaching and writing on sales and sales management and I want to share what I've learned and taught.

Here's what I know. I know that most small-to-medium business owners have had little to no sales or sales management training. You've attended a seminar, watched a webinar, read a book and made some phone calls, but you are not a trained, experienced sales manager.

I also know that you do not have time for theory; you need actionable information, now.

That's what this book is: content you can access and use now. And it is in bite-size bits so you don't have to read forty pages to get an answer. See? Lucky you.

But, lucky me, too. Every day, I get to work with the most creative, motivated, optimistic, expectant, energetic, forward-thinking people I know: small business owners and salespeople. I have the chance daily to impact their lives, to help make their businesses more successful and their futures more secure. .

This book would not have happened without the thumbs-up from Richard Lowe. Don Lowe inspires me, Dan Beck encourages me and I appreciate each of them for their support and friendship.

Denise Denton and Lee Ann Ohanesian assisted with the editing of the chapters and how they are organized. Thank you.

Thanks to Melba Valdez for her cover design.

I am grateful to my teachers. I am indebted to the first one, my mother, who taught me to read and to love to read, before I started school. My life is rich because of it.

From my father I learned to stand up and speak before people.

Miss Ella Mae Jones taught me that I can if I think I can.

Mrs. Corrine Young declared, "Where there's a will, there's a way!"

Coach Andrew Maxey encouraged me to prepare to win, then do my best.

Professor Coleman Raley professed that I should expect perfection from others only when I've achieved it myself.

Professor William Ratliff helped me see that every day is a gift from God and what I do with it is my gift back to Him.

Calvin Miller modeled grace, compassion, creativity and courage.

Gerald Mann affirmed, "Oh, but you *can* begin again."

Zig Ziglar taught that I can have anything I want in life if I'll just help enough other people get what they want.

Brian Tracy accentuated accepting full responsibility for everything. I am responsible.

Alan Cohen taught me to affirm in all circumstances that I am grateful for everything and I have no complaints whatsoever.

Finally, I am humbled by the unwavering support and encouragement of the most important person in my life, Connie. She is the brains and the beauty of this outfit. Lucky me.

First Things First

Only Brain Surgery Is Brain Surgery

Hiring, training, managing and coaching salespeople is not brain surgery.

What's the worst that can happen? You'll fail to find a salesperson or you won't provide training and he/she may fail or you may not manage or coach your salesperson well and he/she may fail or be a perennial underachiever until you have to free the individual up for another opportunity.

Then you start over. No one wants to do that because of the huge amount of time, money and effort spent in the process, and, at the end, you are worse off than in the beginning. But no one dies.

In brain surgery, if things go badly... You know the rest.

Sales management involves these important tasks:

1—Hiring. The sales manager is responsible for recruiting sellers. Always be looking for your next salesperson. You may meet her at a networking event. Maybe you'll meet him in your lobby as he's waiting to meet with one of your colleagues. Or she may come in to sell something to you and you realize what a great fit she would be for your business. Always be looking.

Prior to beginning a formal salesperson search, you should have already determined whether you have the budget, capacity, phone, desk and other requirements for a salesperson. It is also time to construct a salesperson profile and a job description. Then run the ad or contract with the search firm, review resumes and conduct the interviews.

2—Training. Whatever the knowledge and experience level of your new salesperson, you now need to train him to sell for your company. Unless he is trained, how will he know what you do and for whom, what you do most profitably and for what type of customer, the type of work you want to do more or less, payment options, and competitors? Does he have sales skills or need to learn them? Does he know your business or will he need industry and company training? This is also the time to make known your expectations and set performance standards. Training will be an ongoing process to increase knowledge and upgrade skills.

3—Managing. The day-to-day management of your new sales rep will demand a major commitment of your time and that of your staff over the first weeks and months. Daily discussions of her activities and contacts are essential. Quick quizzes on products and services, types of prospects she's been seeing, what they're asking and how she's been answering, what additional information and resources she needs should be a part of your day. You can do it now or do it later, but you'll get better results if you do it early. As with training, managing your salesperson is an ongoing process to achieve maximum results.

4—Coaching. Managing is making sure the right things get done in the right way to the right people, based on your standards of performance. Coaching involves assessing the strengths and weaknesses of your "player," adjusting the game plan, observing performance and

2

evaluating what changes or improvements need to be made. It also involves teaching skills and processes; providing tools and resources to do the job and the opportunity to be successful at it; and motivating your rep with praise and rewards.

The 1972 Miami Dolphins football team is the only NFL team to ever play an entire season with no losses and win the Super Bowl. Their coach, Hall of Famer Don Shula, had a 5-step plan for coaching people, and it is adaptable to sales coaching.

1. Tell people what you want them to do.
2. Show them what good performance looks like.
3. Let them do it.
4. Observe their performance.
5. Praise progress and/or redirect.

"But I'm no Don Shula," you say, "I'm a business owner, not a coach, and I'm not working with highly paid players who represent the best of the best who are realizing their life's dream by playing for me." True, so it is harder. But it isn't brain surgery.

Every successful sales manager started out with the same amount of knowledge and experience you have right now. They learned what they needed to know and practiced it until they reached their current level of ability. You can do this, too.

Part One

Hiring A Salesperson

Reasons to Hire a Salesperson Now

Is now the time for you to take the plunge and hire an outside salesperson? Here are three reasons to go for it, now. What will the right salesperson do for your business?

1—Increase sales from new and existing clients. If you have a sales staff, look back at their first year. On average, how much revenue did your current sellers generate in their first 12 months? What if a new hire did the same thing in his first year? What would that mean to your company in terms of staff, equipment, physical space, operating capital, profitability, etc?

An effective outside rep will sell more to existing accounts, sell a broader range of services to them and have higher average invoices than you see from accounts with no dedicated salesperson.

Customers receiving regular contact from anyone at your company buy more—and more often—than those who do not.

2—Greater visibility in your market. A salesperson is a walking, talking billboard for your company. If he/she simply does some of the sales activities—sales calls, telemarketing calls, qualifying, presenting your capabilities and offers to prospects— even a below-average salesperson will increase awareness of your company and your products or services. That brings you closer to top-of-mind awareness with prospects, and that, likely, will bring more business.

3—Faster rollout of new key services. Someone said, "There are two ways to get to the top of an oak tree. You can climb it or sit on an acorn." You can sell your current offering by phone, direct mail, website and e-mail. But when introducing new products or services, you'll sell them sooner by going to the customer and saying, "Here is a newer/better/faster way to solve your issues. We're already doing this and that for you; how about buying our newest offering?" It is a quicker way to the top of the oak tree.

You may have the greatest whatzit known to man. Do your customers know that? Who will tell them? To make the most of this competitive advantage, you have to go to them and tell your story. It takes a salesperson to do that. That may be you, but it has to be someone.

Even though you may be convinced that the way to build your sales, become more visible and sell additional services is to hire a salesperson, you may be hesitant. There are a number of hard questions to consider, such as: How/where to find a salesperson, how to train and manage him/her, what if you don't get the "right" one the first time, what if yours isn't average, what if the rep leaves in four months, and how much money can you afford to "waste" on a rep that doesn't work out?

It is difficult to find the "right" one. It takes time, money and energy to recruit, hire, train and manage a sales rep and there are no guarantees. There are tools and resources to help you attract better candidates and make better decisions, but there is still some degree of luck involved in finding an exceptional salesperson. There is also risk, but consider the potential payoff.

Are You Ready For A Salesperson?

The decision to hire your first salesperson comes with a lot of questions, including the basic ones: where does one look for a salesperson, what's the hiring process like, what kind of compensation is expected, what are the odds of finding the ideal seller, how does one train the new rep, and what kind of management will it take.

But somewhere between "Do you think you're ready for a salesperson?" and, "When can you start?" there are some other questions you should consider.

• **Can you afford to hire a salesperson?** Many factors go into building a compensation plan. Depending on the size of your business, the industry, your geographical location, the area job market and the type of individual you need, you may expect to pay straight commission, a combination of base salary plus commission or base salary plus bonus. Online resources such as http://www.indeed.com provide salary ranges for sales people and others.

• **Do you have production capacity to support a salesperson?** If you need a rep to generate $450,000 in first-year revenue, you must consider whether you have people and resources to do that much more business. Or are you prepared to add staff and gear as necessary?

• **Do you have room for a salesperson?** Do you have space for her, a desk, telephone and computer? It mustn't be large, but should be at least semi-private, meaning out of traffic and quiet enough for him to make phone calls to customers and prospects.

• **Do you have in-house support for a sales person?** New salespeople tend to generate a lot of proposals and correspondence. Who will do estimates for the rep? Who will write up jobs? Who will manage jobs through delivery? Who will do the quality control? Who will send out the invoices? Who will collect past-due bills?

• **Who will train your salesperson?** There is no shortage of training resources, from in-house experts to weekend seminars or night classes at the community college to national training companies and their websites. The point is that some training must be done on-site, in your location, by you and your employees. Who will do that? Who will tell him what you produce in-house and what you buy out? Who will train him regarding prospects and customers and opportunities in your trade area?

• **Who will manage your salesperson?** It cannot be outsourced and you will not reap the benefits of your sales effort if sales management is ignored. You or someone in your business must manage the salesperson. At the very least, that means ensuring that he has the training, tools and time to be successful. It also means setting goals, defining activities and then ensuring that they are done.

So, are you ready for a salesperson?

Where Will You Find Your Salesperson?

Always be recruiting, because you never know where or when you'll find your sales rep. More than one has been found in the lobby of a print shop, copying their resume. Here's a list of other ways to discover your seller.

• **Look among your staff** – Several excellent salespeople have come from the administrative, customer service and production areas. You'll have to rehire for the position they're leaving and teach them to sell, but your new seller will get off to a faster start because of her knowledge of your industry, your customers and capabilities.

• **Word of mouth** – This is the best and least expensive way. Tell everyone you know that you're looking for a sales rep. Tell your employees, friends, neighbors, customers and vendors that you're looking, and the type of salesperson you're hoping to find. Someone may know someone who knows someone.

• **Advertise** – Place a free or low-cost ad online on CraigsList.com, CareerBuilder.com or Monster.com. Try industry, trade association or college and university websites. Your local or regional newspaper is a less-desirable option, as most people seeking sales jobs will go online.

• **Your college's job placement center or job board** is a fine place if you're looking for an entry-level salesperson. There are a number of advantages to going this way – the low cost of recruiting being one – but your work is cut out for both of you. You may be hiring someone who doesn't know anything about your product/service or about selling. Most likely, they also don't know how to work.

• **Employment agency** – This is the most expensive option, as you will be required to pay the agency a fee equal to some percentage (as high as 25-30%) of the new hire's first-year salary. In exchange, the agency runs the search, does the initial screening and presents you with only qualified candidates. Some agencies offer guarantees.

• **Headhunter** – For highly-skilled, high-quality, experienced salespeople, this is the way to go. The headhunter may conduct a nationwide search and do all the screening. You will pay a significant fee to the headhunter, but you will get what you want.

The process of recruiting begins with assessing your situation to decide whether you can hire a salesperson, then considering where you'll find one. Next we'll look at the type of salesperson you'll hire and how to pay them.

Hiring a Salesperson

If you've decided to hire a sales person, here are six suggestions to help you get off to a good start.

1—Set expectations. In the interview process, let the candidate know how performance is measured: by sales activities, revenue goals or a combination of the two. It is a mistake to ask any employee to hit a non-existent target.

2—Get expectations. Find out what the candidate expects to get out of this job: training, experience, money, awards, a career, etc. The answer will help you know how to motivate him/her in the future.

3—Negotiate expectations. Chances are that neither you nor the candidate will get everything you want in this partnership. Define the non-negotiable points and get agreement to them. Or, agree that this may not be the right opportunity for him/her.

4—Tell your new salesperson how he/she is to bring value to your company through productivity and through awareness of the needs of internal and external customers. Show the new hire the steps involved and the resources available to get the job done.

5—Observe FOCUS: the Fundamentals Of Concentrating Under Stress. This will help both of you survive the difficulties that are sure to arise in the sales rep/manager relationship. Remain FOCUSed on achieving the agreed upon expectations.

6—Inspect what you expect. Measure performance and reward achievement. Identify deficiencies, and prescribe a course for getting back on track.

How To Hire A Winner Every Time

If I could hire a winner every time, I would have written this book years ago and I'd sell it for a fantastical amount of money. I would now be lying in a hammock strung between two palm trees on my own, private island in the Caribbean, not thinking about you. Fact is, I cannot hire a winner every time and neither can anyone else.

I know *how* to hire a winner every time; I just don't do it, and neither do you.

WHY WE DON'T
There are dozens of reasons for hiring mistakes, whether that means someone who fails or someone who fails to measure up to expectations. Things like:

• **Hiring quickly** to fill an open position because "it's better to have someone than no one out there."
• **Falling in love** with a candidate because of personality, appearance, resume or superb interviewing skills.
• **Hiring the best** of a bad bunch.
• **Hiring because you can** get them cheap, they can start immediately and they seem really excited about the job.
• **Insert your own reason here.**

Now, the HOW TO
1. Identify the personal traits, behaviors and motivators necessary for doing the job in a satisfactory manner and

create a customized job benchmark to identify those individuals who are a good fit for the job.

An online search for the term *traits of top salespeople* may result in more than 200-thousand hits, and perhaps that many different lists of traits. They are the general traits of the best reps and they will always include terms like: *highly assertive, people-oriented, impatient, independent, energetic logical thinkers.*

You'll also find: *they are skilled at prospecting and closing; they respond positively to incentives and commissions; they are not detail oriented; and they are self-motivated, neither wanting nor needing much direction.*

Any sales job requires prospecting, qualifying, presenting, closing and follow-up. A salesperson must cold call, telemarket, get appointments, ask questions, offer solutions, ask for the business and follow-up with the prospect until he becomes a customer. That's the job.

2. Cull the candidates who are not a good fit for your sales position, even if they have previous sales experience, even if it is within your industry. That your product or service is of use to people with specific technical skills means your sales rep must know, or be able to learn, how to talk their language.

Do you sell to big business or mom and pop? Private or public companies? Government agencies or universities? You must hire accordingly.

Don't presume that previous sales experience, even in like markets and products, was positive and productive or that they are motivated and have good selling skills or that they will fully apply them in your business.

3. Separate the interview stars from those who have the personal skills and motivational style that fit the job. Don't fall in love with a candidate because she looks good, he says all the right things, she asks great questions, he asks for the job, she sends a thank you note, etc. You're looking for someone with the right personal skills, customer focus, accountability, self-management and the rest, who fits the job.

4. Hire the best one, based on the resume, interviews, pre-hire tests, references and any other tools available to you. If you do everything right, which is seldom, you'll hire a winner. If you do just some things right, your odds go up.

The Profile of a Top Performer

Thinking of hiring a salesperson? I know what you're looking for—a superstar. You're hoping to find the next Rookie of the Year.

So, should you look for a man or woman, and should they be younger or older? The answer, in both cases, may be yes.

One company with which I worked had 52 reps who qualified for the Top Performers Club. There were 27 women and 25 men, ranging in age from about 30 to 60-something. They had been selling at the company for between 3 and 20-plus years. Some of them had grown up in this industry, but had no sales experience or industry background when hired.

One had been a flight attendant, one had taught school, and one was a printing press operator. There were marrieds and singles, parents and grandparents. One was an artist; one was a competitive cyclist. They came from big cities and small towns, from Anchorage to Tampa and from California to New York. Each one was different but they shared some common traits.

When they took the online test operators give to sales candidates, they revealed their success traits. We learned that there were six specific traits these individuals share, though not everyone had them to the same degree.

From this, we can extrapolate that an applicant who takes the same test and reveals the same traits has the appearance of a future Top Performer. It is not a guarantee, but it is an indication, and that's better than a guess.

Here are the six traits common to these Top Performers:

1. Assertiveness – Strength, fortitude, steadiness and competitiveness
2. Independence – Self-reliant, neither needing nor desiring much direction
3. Hunter/Closer Mentality – Actively seeking additional business and working, with purpose, toward securing it
4. Sense of urgency – Impatience, restlessness, with a bias for action
5. Results-orientation – Focused on outcomes, not activities
6. Incentive-orientation – Preferring opportunity to security, responding to challenges in pursuit of a prize

They are the same traits high achievers have in any sales organization. Top Performers are assertive, independent "hunters" for additional business, impatient and eager to land it and achieve their goals because they want the rewards that come with achievement. As you consider your current salesperson(s) and future candidates, this is the model.

Now for a dose of reality. Not every salesperson will be a Top Performer. In any organization, there will be the top 20 percent, who excel; the 60 percent of average performers; and 20 percent who are underachievers.

Using any personality/style profile test will increase your odds of hiring an individual with the traits that make him likely to succeed.

How to Hire a Solution Seller

The bulk of your revenue last year came from what we call simple sales: regular orders or reorders of products or projects for regular clients, placed by a lower-level person in the organization, doing all at little risk to either party. You and your customer service representatives do it all day long, asking simple questions about delivery or pickup, Tuesday or Thursday, cash or credit. That's what we mean by simple sales.

Some of your sales are complex ones, meaning that there are two or more parts or processes to the job. Some components are produced in-house, some bought out or use outside services or are ordered by two or more people, perhaps at a higher level in the organization. Often these are projects that have never been done before, so you get involved in consulting regarding design, process, size, colors, etc. They cost more and carry more risk to you and your customer than so-called simple or commodity products.

With proper training and the desire to succeed, a salesperson can do very well at the simple sale in a matter of months. But the complex sale requires more training and a different approach to selling. The sales cycle is longer; there are more elements involved in the process, maybe a buying team or committee and multiple meetings.

Many salespeople can learn to sell solutions, but some are reluctant to learn something new and leave their simple-selling zones. Some will not learn the skills for gaining access to and selling to higher-level decision-makers. Some cannot adjust to the longer selling cycle.

If you're looking to add a salesperson now, you may want to focus your efforts on finding someone who can sell solutions. How would one go about that?

Identify Your Hiring Criteria
You are looking for a salesperson who can build credibility with prospects, move prospects through the sales cycle, ensure customer success and build on that relationship. To discover that kind of salesperson, you will need to look for their proven ability to deliver on sales goals, meaning you won't hire a rookie. You'll want someone who can define a market and take a value-based sales approach, focused on revenue and margins, not on lowest cost. He/she will need to be able to understand decision-makers and identify their pains, match solutions to problems, and clearly communicate their proposals to prospects and customers.

Ask Specific Questions
Develop questions that will yield useful information on specific examples instead of generalities. For example:

- How do you sell a solution? Walk me through the process.
- How do/did you select accounts to focus on?
- How do you build credibility with different decision-makers?
- How do you learn about/assess a customer's circumstances and objectives?
- Who are some high-level executives you've sold to and how did you get in to see them and develop a relationship with them?
- How do you demonstrate a solution's value to a potential decision maker?

- How long can it take you to close a deal?
- What was your role after the sale was made?

Look For Red Flags
- If the candidate cannot articulate the business value of a solution...
- If he/she cannot give details about how he or she closed a deal...
- If the interviewee reverts to discussing features, volume and price...
- If he/she is unable to detail his/her previous successes...
- If what the candidate says doesn't match the résumé...
  ...move on to the next candidate.

Where to Find Candidates for Solution Selling
Your current salesperson may be able to learn to sell solutions. Maybe you have a knowledgeable, talented employee who does not work in sales but who understands how to ask questions and explain the value of your offering. You may choose to give him the opportunity.

 If you look outside your company, account executives from suppliers, competitors or even neighbors may already have the training and skills to be a solution seller. Industry job banks may work for you. Monster.com, CareerBuilder.com and the other major sites should be considered, as well as your city/state job postings on Craig's List (www.craigslist.com). Employment agency or headhunter fees can be high, but they are worth it if you find the right person.

Hiring a Solution Seller

The word *solution* surely has become one of the most overused and misused words in these early years of the 21st century.

One year, a large grocery chain in my area ran a full-color ad hyping its "Valentine's Celebration Solutions." Imagine, *solutions* for the big day! Oh, their solutions were roses and chocolates, of course, but also on the cover of the ad section were photos of fish and chips, key lime pie and sweetheart cookies. Honestly, would those things solve any problems with your love life?

In this column, we'll discuss how to find a solution seller, the salesperson of the present and future. First, let's define solution selling.

What is Solution Selling?
Our definition is: an offering, made up of different components, which is proposed to resolve some specific issue(s) that a customer or prospect is experiencing.

The starting point is the customer issue, rather than the offering itself. Solution selling may result in the sale of product, but it would not be cost-effective to approach the solution this way.

Solution selling begins with finding out what needs or priorities the customer or prospect has, then coming back with an offer combining two, three or more components to meet those needs or priorities, at what the customer perceives as a value.

The first step is investigation, determining whether a prospect will buy anything and, if so, what and whether they will buy it from you.

The next step is a needs analysis, finding out which problems cry out for a solution, determining whether you have the components to address the need or desire, and then presenting a comprehensive answer. That answer should be presented in such a way that the prospect would have to be a fool to not allow you to ease his pain.

The third step is to give a plan that meets the objectives, shows the proof that you're meeting them and look for additional opportunities.

If what I've just described made you think of a suite of products and services, you are correct. Trade show display packages, A/V equipment or signage are products. A program that involves increasing your customer's sales by drawing prospects into her booth, showing the value of her goods, and having those packages assembled and drop-shipped to customer locations, at a profit, is a solution.

Who is a Solution Seller?
There is a difference between a product pusher and a solution seller. A big difference.

A solution seller has skills a peddler does not have. They include the ability to think abstractly, to ask questions and hear the answers, to imagine possibilities, to draw in resources from diverse sources and to communicate the result in such a way that the customer sees, hears and feels a resolution.

A solution seller assesses the opportunity presented by a specific prospect, researches what problems, issues and initiatives the prospect has, quantifies the cost of fixing/not fixing the issues and offers a solution that provides more value than the cost of implementing it, delivers and then looks for more opportunities. Such a seller costs more than you may be willing to pay and may take longer than you're willing to wait for results.

How to Hire a Solution Salesperson
First, know what you're looking for – a problem-solver, not a product pusher.

Second, ask questions that elicit stories, like, "Tell me about the greatest value you've ever delivered to a customer. What did you do that made them want to adopt you?" And listen.

Next, allow the salesperson the time and resources to investigate, think, imagine, locate sources, penetrate the buyer's defenses, create an ally or sponsor, present and close the business.

Fourth, provide opportunities for them to learn how to sell solutions.

Finally, you'll need to transition from a product sales manager to a solution sales manager.

The Salesperson of the Future

You already know why you should have an outside sales presence, how to find one. We have addressed how to help your salesperson grow into who he/she needs to be to meet the needs of your business.

You are painfully aware that your business has changed significantly over the past few years. Hardly any segment looks like it did five years ago, so you are continually updating business plans, marketing tools, equipment and personnel. The years ahead promise more challenges, and so you will continue to change or you will not survive.

That applies to your outside sales program as well. As you lead your company, plan for upgrades to your sales staff. Changes in the marketplace as well as in your product and service offerings will demand that your outside salespeople be more knowledgeable and more professional in their approach to selling. What does that mean to you?

A Different Kind of Salesperson

That may call for hiring a different salesperson or for helping your current one get smarter and more professional. Making friends and building relationships will always be the bedrock of sales success, but the salesperson of the future will need more than a stack of leads and business cards to remain relevant to your customers. They are getting smarter, too, and so are the salespeople in their companies, so they will have greater expectations of yours.

The salesperson of the future must have sales skills, relationship skills and be comfortable with digital technology. To succeed in the coming years, your rep will move from selling your current offering to selling solutions to customers' problems. If your rep is still counting on "a shoeshine and a smile," like Willy Loman in *Death of a Salesman,* his future is not bright. Either your seller must grow or you'll have to make a change.

A Different Kind of Sales Management

It follows, then, that how you hire, train and manage must also transition from a commodity-selling approach to solution selling. You won't stop measuring activities and dollars, but the activities will be more than cold calls, telemarketing calls and appointments. As your rep learns how to have better conversations with higher-level people in the organization, you'll learn to measure things like call plans, questions, processes and advances. And you may be looking for a "better" salesperson, who will cost more and who should deliver greater results, but who may take longer than you'd like to do so. In fact, it takes longer to sell a solution than an order.

The Have-to-Haves of Selling

Like all of us, your salesperson sometimes confuses niceties with necessities. I know this. They talk to me.

They tell me things like, "I could sell a lot more IF...
 "...we had a new Whiz Bang in house."
 "...I had an office of my own."
 "...I didn't have to share the computer with the CSR."
 "...my boss would do regular mailings to my
     prospects."
 "...my boss would give me some good leads."
 "...I had a tablet computer so I could do design and
     quotes on the spot."
 "...my boss would be a little more flexible on pricing."

I agree with them that it would be nice to have whatever it is they're missing, but I can point to real people in every business who have become successful at selling without that nice thing.

You probably have a list of things it would be nice to have to grow your business, don't you? I have my own list.

When I talk with new salespeople, I tell them, "There are five things you absolutely must have or acquire if you are going to be successful at selling. Without them your bank account will be empty, your spouse will be cranky, your kids will be skinny, your dog will growl at you, your brother-in-law will call you a loser, your neighbors will sneer at you, David Letterman will ridicule you on national television, your feet will stink and you will be doomed to a lifetime of wishing you could have the things you cannot afford for your family."

27

There are lots of things it would be nice to have, but these five things are the have-to haves:

- **Something to Sell.** Does your company sell products and services everyone buys, like clothing, groceries, tires, office supplies, etc.? Or does it sell tray tables for private aircraft? Is that product line sustainable, meaning, can your company exist and grow for the forseeable future without adding additional products/services? And, in either case, are your current salespeople selling all you have to sell?

- **Someone to Sell It To.** It is the job of the salesperson to go out into the offices, factories and warehouses where products like yours are being used every day and find prospects to sell to. Everyone is a suspect until they qualify as a prospect: those with the want or need, money and authority to buy what you sell, who indicate they might be willing to buy it from you. Is your salesperson spending adequate time prospecting and qualifying prospects to develop into customers?

- **A Unique Sales Presentation.** In his book *No B.S. Business Success*, Dan Kennedy asks, "Has it ever occurred to you that the reason you're having trouble getting past gatekeepers, the reason your mailings don't get response, and the reason your customers aren't referring others to you in waves may be that YOU ARE BORING?" If your salesperson prospects, leaves voice-mail messages, sends e-mails and writes letters like every other salesperson, there's lots of competition. If your rep is out selling your wares based on quality-service-price, what makes him/her different from anyone else? Do something different! Ask questions, and offer solutions.

- **The Ability to Close the Sale.** The best salesperson with the most dynamic presentation delivered to the right prospect can fail, nonetheless, unless he/she has the courage to ask for the business. Everyone is expecting some sort of close. "Well, whaddya think?" is not it. Salespeople must learn to bring the sales conversation to its logical conclusion, restating the issues raised by the prospect with his/her proposed solution(s) and asking questions like, "Does that make sense? Where do we go from here? How would you like me to proceed? What do you see as the next step? When shall we meet to cover the details? Whom else shall we share this with?" Salespeople who do not close are not salespeople; they are conversationalists. Can your salesperson actually close the deal?

- **A Follow-up System.** Eighty percent of all sales are made after the fifth attempt, but most salespeople give up after two or three attempts to get the sale. People do business with people they know, like and trust. That takes time. Diligent follow-up with qualified prospects is the answer, and that requires a system.

  Want it on a bumper sticker? **See the right people the right number of times**. That's the answer. Maintaining a weekly or biweekly schedule of follow-ups, using direct mail, e-mail, phone calls, personal visits, small gifts and personal notes—all of these working together to build relationships. Is your salesperson a serial prospector? That could be the problem. Does he/she do the diligent follow-up needed?

Recruiting and Hiring Mistakes—Part I

At any gathering where the topic of hiring a salesperson comes up, someone has a bad experience to share. Employing a salesperson that will be successful takes equal parts of time, effort, skill and luck. Whether you're a full-time sales manager or an owner/sales manager, hiring for the first or fourth time, there are a number of costly mistakes you want to avoid. Let's look at several of them:

- **Hiring the best of a bad bunch**
  It is more critical than ever before to hire a salesperson, if your business is to grow. But it is more important that you get the right one. Because of the investment in time and money (up to three times the annual salary of the salesperson), you don't want to go through the hiring process every year. If, after reviewing the résumés and/or concluding the interview process, you're not satisfied with the results, place another ad, talk to more contacts, ask for more referrals and begin the process again. While this takes time, in the end you will save time, money and frustration by not hiring a bad candidate.

- **Hiring under pressure and making snap judgments**
  At this writing, we're in an employers market and there may be plenty of qualified candidates for your sales position. Take your time when making a hiring decision. If you feel pressured to make a decision on a candidate before you are ready, either because of the fear of losing the candidate or because of a low

response rate, you could end up hiring a mistake. Have a partner or several key employees conduct a second interview with the candidate, and then evaluate him/her based on all of the input. You will be adding the salesperson to your mix of existing employees, and a bad hire can have a negative effect on the whole team.

- **Hiring people we like because it is comfortable and less threatening**
  Be certain you're hiring a person whose skills and characteristics match your needs. Once you determine which skills are important for a candidate, don't deviate from them. Employ a salesperson you can work with on a daily basis, with the skills and characteristics you require, and you will have a greater chance for success. Deviate from those skills and characteristics, and you'll have someone you won't want in a matter of months.

- **Not networking, not keeping files, not adopting a continuous process**
  One of the best ways to avoid hiring under pressure or hiring the best of a bad bunch is to always be recruiting. That way, you'll have a pool of successful salespeople to draw from. Perhaps they were among your first choices in a previous search, but were not available at that time. In addition to keeping files, let your vendors, customers and friends know that you are always looking for a good salesperson. This will promote a flow of referrals. If you put into place a continuous process of recruiting, you should never have to struggle to replace or add to your sales team.

- **Not systematically upgrading the sales force through continuous improvement**
  The better the selling skills of your salesperson, the more effective he/she will be in all aspects of the sales process. In order to be a top performer, your salesperson must be committed to improvement: learning the selling skills in which he/she is weak, learning new and better processes and learning advanced selling techniques. If you consistently push your salespeople to improve, they will determine that you want them to succeed, and that you are supporting them in their efforts. In turn, you'll have a higher performing sales team.

- **Not using a variety of sources**
  Use several different methods to generate candidates, such as online job postings, word of mouth and networking. This process will assure a mix of candidates. Ask for referrals from everyone that you know because a salesperson with a personal recommendation is generally a good hire.

Recruiting and Hiring Mistakes—Part II

Whether you are a full-time sales manager or a business owner, and whether you're hiring for the first or fourth time, there are a number of costly mistakes to avoid when hiring a salesperson. In Part I we discussed six of them: Hiring the best of a bad bunch; Hiring under pressure and making snap judgments; Hiring people we like because it is comfortable and less threatening; Not networking, not keeping files, not adopting a continuous process; Not continually upgrading the sales force through continuous improvement; Not using a variety of sources. Here are six more mistakes:

- **Not checking references**
  It is difficult, if not impossible, to gather any in-depth information on a candidate from previous employers, but it is important to at least try. In most cases, they will only verify employment, dates, position and compensation, though some companies and personal references are more open to a conversation. You may learn about inconsistencies, habits and the way this person is perceived, all of which will assist you in your hiring decision. Always ask if the individual is eligible for rehire. At the very least, you'll learn whether the information on the résumé was correct.

- **Not asking probing questions**
  Just as salespeople are taught to ask questions to learn about a prospect, you should create a list of questions to ask your sales candidates. Probing questions are those that begin with, "Tell me about a

time..." or " Give me an example of..." These types of questions require the candidate to pull their responses from real-life experiences, rather than from learned or practiced responses. Probing questions also give you an idea of how the candidate would react in real-world situations. Some salespeople, by the nature of their career, are excellent at selling themselves in the interview process, but fall short when it's time to perform the actual job. These types of questions will reveal which type of candidate you are interviewing.

- **Talking too much during the interview**
  During the interview, your goal should be to get to know the candidate. The candidate's goal is to learn about you and your business. Whoever does the most listening is going to learn the most. Since your objective is to get to know the individual and his/her qualifications, the most effective process is through questioning. If you don't ask thought-provoking and probing questions, you'll only know them by the information that is on the resume. Ideally, you'll talk only 20 percent of the time. So, ask your questions. Then sit back, listen to their responses and take notes.

- **Not preparing a job description or candidate profile**
  Developing a candidate profile will help you determine what skills and characteristics are important for your salesperson. Use it when you place your ad (list your top three skills as requirements for hiring), during the interview ask questions that focus on the skills and characteristics you've chosen, and when you make the final hiring

decision, be certain this candidate has what you're looking for in a salesperson.

Creating a job description prior to the interview will prevent you from hiring a salesperson who will not cold call, enter contact information into ACT!, or attend morning meetings. The job description is a roadmap of primary and secondary responsibilities for the salesperson to follow. It should also be used during their evaluations to determine whether or not they're doing the job.

During the interview process, ask the candidate to review the job's responsibilities. If something is pointed out as a problem, consider that this may not be your ideal candidate. Once you hire, present the job description again, on the salesperson's first day. Each party should sign it, acknowledging agreement to it. Then retain a copy for performance evaluations.

- **Not matching the candidate to buyer behavior, type of selling, or sales process:** relationship selling, consultative selling, closer, detailer, order-taker, partnership selling, application selling.

There are a number of different types of sales, and there are personality types for every type. In many cases they are not interchangeable. Solution selling is both relationship and consultative. This type of selling requires relationship building, the persistence of calling on a prospect 10 to 13 times, and being able to suggest new or better ways of doing projects. An order-taker will be used to pointing out what is currently on promotion, but is not used to selling consultatively or guiding the buyer. He/she is used to writing an order every time and selling on discount. A detailer builds a relationship, shows features and benefits, but doesn't close a sale. A closer is someone who takes one opportunity to close or lose the deal, so he/she will use hard-sell tactics. The hard-sell closer may be thrown out of the prospect's office, the order-taker will only close a sale if the prospect buys on relationship, and the detailer will only close by accident. To be successful, it is important to match the personality of your salesperson to our type of sales.

- **Not terminating weak performers: not weeding the garden**
A top performer is a salesperson who has been properly trained and managed, has realistic goals, and has been given enough time to generate the business needed to achieve his/her objective. Not every salesperson will be a top performer. In fact, in any sales organization, only 20 percent will be. But if your plan calls for a $350,000 a year salesperson, and your rep is still selling $140,000 after two years, it's time to look for someone who is more in line with your plan and who will help you achieve your goals. When you keep a weak performer, he/she may drag down the rest of your team, as well as be a drain on your finances.

Avoiding these 12 costly mistakes in recruiting and hiring will save time, money and frustration. In addition, you'll avoid the stress of looking for a new salesperson, and make better hiring decisions.

Time To Add Another Salesperson?

When should I add another salesperson?
Should I look for another one like my current rep?
How do I divide the territory between them?
Do I give the new guy house accounts to get
started?
Can I have my salesperson train the new one?

Have you thought about adding to your sales staff? There are a number of benefits to having two or more salespeople. One is the increased revenue anticipated in a new rep's first year. Also, two reps equal a sales team for synergy, competition, sharing of best practices and trading of prospects with whom one is getting nowhere. Sales meetings feel more comfortable and productive when you meet with more than a single salesperson. One salesperson's good month may compensate for the other's bad month. And, when one salesperson leaves, you have one to carry on the business while you rehire.

Let's consider some questions regarding hiring an additional salesperson for a company.

Why should I add another salesperson? There's only one good reason: to grow profitable sales.

When is it time to hire another sales rep?
• When you want or need to grow profitable sales and your salesperson cannot do any more. In most cases, your rep can do more, if he/she wants to and if you have systems to make it possible. For example, the more customers your rep has on an online ordering system,

the less time is spent on servicing them. After such efforts, though, when your salesperson is truly at his/her limit, it may be time to hire an additional salesperson.

• When your salesperson doesn't want to increase sales anymore. Just like business owners, salespeople find their comfort zone, where they are meeting their goals and making enough money, they are happy with their client list and they aren't working too many hours. They do just enough prospecting and new account development to stay even.

• When you commit to take your business to another level, one to which your salesperson is not trained or equipped to go. If your current sales rep does not have the interest or ability to learn what he/she needs to know to sell some new offering, you'll need to hire one who knows, or who will learn, to sell more sophisticated products or services.

How should we divide the territory? In some cases, geographic territories make sense. In others, industry or product niches would be better. In most cases, no division is necessary. Through regular meetings and good communication, conflicts and duplication of activities can be avoided.

What kind of salesperson should I look for now? Someone compatible but different from your current salesperson. Hire a woman to complement your sales man; hire younger to complement maturity; hire enthusiasm to complement stability; hire knowledge to complement energy. Each person will challenge and motivate the other. Each will secure customers the other could not.

Should I give the new rep some house accounts to get started? Probably. A salesperson's customer list is the greatest assurance you have that someone is actually doing customer development. In most companies where the owner is not active in selling, house accounts are taken for granted until they go away. Select twenty house accounts with potential and turn them over to the new salesperson to develop.

Should my current salesperson train the new hire? Be careful with that. Unless you are completely delighted with everything your current salesperson does, he/she is not the best trainer. You are. Train your new rep your way, and then have him/her ride with the veteran and observe how she does it. Point out the differences and make your expectations known. You are the manager.

Part Two

Training A Salesperson

Everybody Sells!

Quick! What do these people have in common: Donald Trump, Harvey Mackay, Bill Marriott, Walt Disney, Colonel Sanders, Suzanne Sommers, Michael Ovitz, Zig Ziglar, Marie Osmond, Tony Robbins, Ron Popeil, Jeffrey Hayzlett, Barry Farber, Jeffrey Gitomer, Joan Rivers, David Oreck, Bill Clinton, Hillary Clinton, Sarah Palin, Barak Obama?

Every one is a salesperson and all of us sell every day, whether we're selling a spouse on going to see the movie we want to see, selling a child on cleaning his room, selling the police officer on why we edged just above the speed limit.

Even you and every member of your staff, from your procurement director and IT manager to the delivery driver, everybody sells. And in these uncertain days, when customers go out of business unexpectedly, price-shop every job and order from you less frequently and in smaller quantities, everybody *must* sell.

Like virtually every company, one of your business objectives is to increase sales by selling more to existing customers. You want to sell greater quantities and additional items to those buyers who know you best and trust you most. And you want to help them sell more to their customers.

Whether you call it this or not, the term is *cross-sell/upsell*. It means selling additional items, complimentary, higher quality or more effective items. You are being cross-sold/upsold every day, from McDonalds' "Would you like fries with that?" to Wendy's "Want to biggie-size it?" to 7-11's "Need a lighter, too? Batteries?"

When a regular customer calls or comes into your printing firm and places an order for 5,000 #10 envelopes, there are two ways you or your customer service reps may handle that order.

In the first case, get the specs, deadline and payment information and thank them for the order. You print the envelopes, deliver them, send the invoice, get the check and deposit it. That works, and you're happy to do that all day long.

But consider this. If you've trained your staff to be curious and ask questions, the CSR gets the specs, deadline and payment information on the envelopes, then says, "Looks like you're going to be mailing lots of letters. Do you have enough letterhead?" Here are some additional *cross-sell/upsell* questions:

"Are these going to customers or prospects?
"Will you enclose business cards? Have enough
 for the project?
"Anything else going in the envelope?
"How'd you like us to do the stuffing and mailing,
too? We do that for many of our customers."

By asking a few simple questions, your rep may prompt
the buyer to order additional, complimentary items to
go with the original one, increasing the amount of the
sale, his commission and your profit.

Train the delivery driver, too. He can ask questions such
as, "Man, that's a lot of envelopes. You're not going to
address and stuff all of them yourself, are you? We can
do that for you." Or, "Are you going to be doing several
of these projects? You could get a better price by
ordering a larger quantity next time."

From the larger perspective, you and your salespeople
need to learn to ask questions about business objectives,
including lead generation, customer retention, customer
reactivation, brand extension and more. Knowing more
about our customers' priorities prepares us to offer
solutions to help them succeed. That's good for
everyone.

Salespeople are trained in *cross-sell/upsell* tactics, but
anyone else who has customer contact should be, too.
Be curious, not nosey. Ask questions and offer
suggestions. Selling is everybody's job, especially now.
Train everybody to sell.

Things You Can Do Something About

> *God, grant me the serenity*
> *To accept the things I cannot change,*
> *Courage to change the things I can,*
> *And the wisdom to know the difference.*

Is there anyone who has not seen or heard this verse before? The Serenity Prayer, as it is known, is printed on cards, sewn on pillows, etched in stone and spoken daily by participants in 12-step programs, believers and nonbelievers alike. Its origin is uncertain, but it is generally accepted to have been written by theologian Reinhold Niebuhr.

Read it again. Do you think serenity comes from accepting the things you cannot change or from changing the things you can? Or both? Since this is not a discussion of theology or etymology, let's focus on a practical application of the verse as it relates to sales and sales management.

In working with hundreds of people who have come into selling with no prior background, I find it interesting to find out how much they seem to "know." Wherever they learned it, many new salespeople subscribe to various sales laws, including:

- **The Law of Numbers:** Selling is purely a numbers game. Talk to enough people, and some will buy from you.
- **The Law of the Jungle:** It's a jungle out there; it's kill or be killed.
- **The Law of Knowledge:** The one with the most information wins.

- **The Law of the Low Price:** Price is all that matters. Sharpen your pencil, get competitive, come in with the lowest price and everyone will buy from you.
- **The Law of the Unique Market:** My market's different. People here don't care about value, they buy strictly on price, and they don't go on the Internet.
- **The Law of the Whale:** Go after the big customers. One whale equals millions of minnows. Don't fool with the small stuff.
- **The Law of Lock and Load:** If I could use a gun, I could get people to buy. (Don't try this. I live in Texas and even here, it is against the law to use guns to sell.)

There is some truth in each of these, but none is the law of selling—unless your sales rep thinks it is. And what do you do then, sales manager?

I suggest you lead your salesperson in the serenity prayer and set about to change what you can, accept what you cannot change, and ask for the wisdom to know the difference.

Like dealing with objections. Rookie sales reps, especially, tend to get completely flustered when an objection is raised by a prospect. I know I did. When a prospect dared to challenge my statement that our product was the best, our service was outstanding and our prices were fair, I was stunned and did not know how to react. I had no comeback. I'd drop my head, tuck my tail and slink off to my next cold call, hoping to not encounter another objection. But that was no way to make a living and I had to come up with a strategy for dealing with objections. Let me share it with you in hopes that you will practice it and share it with your sales reps.

1—In a meeting with your salesperson, write down every objection he/she is hearing. There are only a few of them and sales reps hear them over and over. Here are the most common ones:

- We already have a supplier we're happy with.
- Your prices are too high.
- We don't use outside vendors. We do everything in-house.
- We have to order everything from headquarters.
- Your parts won't work in our machines.

Now ask yourself, are those viable objections? If not to you, are they viable to your salesperson? If so, how does he/she respond to them? How would you respond to them? Is there anything you can do to make them go away? Can you change them or must you accept them? Do you know the difference?

2—Do this exercise with your rep(s): Talk about the objections and brainstorm some responses. How would you answer the price objection or "We do everything in-house?" Come up with a good answer or two or three and write them out. Over the next week, memorize them. Do that for each objection, and you will never have to fumble around for a response or run and hide again.

Once you're comfortable handling those objections, take the next step. Learn to respond to them in a way that will lead you toward opportunity. Accept the fact that, when you attempt to sell, you will get objections. Change how you respond to them. Wisdom. Courage. Serenity.

Objections Are Not Deal Killers

In his prime, Zig Ziglar was the best-known sales trainer in the world. The man from Yazoo City, Mississippi learned to sell the hard way, selling cookware. The process involved door-to-door cold calling in residential areas during the day, setting up appointments to come back one evening and cook supper for the family and a few friends. Meal preparation was a demonstration of the pots and pans; the meal itself was the payoff for the prospect. When everyone had enjoyed the most delicious, nutritious meal ever—and it was free!—Zig would attempt to close the sale of the cookware to the host family and to their guests.

He was not an overnight success. He experienced frustration and failure until he met an older, more experienced salesman who shared with him a selling system. Over time, he improved it, then perfected it and it made him wealthy and famous in his industry. Then he started teaching others to sell, travelling the world, teaching and inspiring salespeople.

One of the things I learned from him is that whenever two people get together for a sales discussion, someone's going to sell something. Either the salesperson will sell his product to the prospect or the prospect will sell the salesperson on why he can't or won't buy what the salesperson is selling.

An essential part of learning to sell is learning to deal with objections. New salespeople, especially, tend to see an objection as the end of the selling process, rather than as a step in it. If the prospect gives an objection, many salespeople will give in or give up on the sale.

How can you help your salesperson deal with the inevitable objections? Here is a system you can share with your seller.

Having identified the most common objections and preparing answers for them, be careful how you say them so you don't come off as being hostile or indifferent. There is a reason why prospects give a specific objection, and it is important to them, so treat it that way.

One of the oldest and best ways to respond to an objection is with the three-step formula: *feel-felt-found*. It may be used with several of the usual objections.

Suppose a prospect says, "Your prices are too high." Using *feel-felt-found*, you might respond this way: "I understand how you *feel*. Several of my best customers *felt* the same way before they started working with us. What they've *found* is that the service we provide, and the convenience of working with a full-service company, more than justify the few dollars more we might charge on a specific project."

What if your prospect says, "We've been with Mission Software for five years and we're very happy with them." Your salesperson could reply, "I understand how you *feel* about your trusted vendor. You know, every one of my current customers *felt* that way when I began calling on them. What they've *found* is that my company offers the added benefit of automatic backup and upgrades, and that simplifies their life."

You'll think of additional ways to counter objections. Write them out.

Most importantly, think of an objection as a request for more information, and give it. The selling process isn't over just because someone raises an objection.

Third, memorize the three responses to each objection. Review them regularly so that you or your salesperson will not be caught searching for words when you hear the objection. You'll have a well-thought-out, reasoned response.

Fourth, keep current with added products and services. You'll get new objections when you bring up some new offerings. As you hear those objections, write them down, write out three responses, memorize and review them frequently. Be prepared!

As you train new salespeople and work with experienced salespeople to help them become more successful, remember to train them on responding to objections.

Solution Selling Training

You now know that there are two ways to have a solution salesperson on your staff. You can hire one or train your current salesperson to sell solutions. Maybe.

Some sales reps "get it" right away. Some, on their own, realize there is more to life than capturing the low hanging fruit and decide to go after a higher class of business. That means selling to higher level buyers with bigger problems, who can and will spend more dollars to solve them.

Million Dollar Club members figured this out and, by trial and error, changed the way they sell. It affected how they prospect, how they present, the kind of customers they have and the kind of work they do for them. In most cases, they have fewer customers who buy more from them. It is very likely that a salesperson who has been with you for more than two years and hasn't figured this out is not going to do so on his/her own, but needs to be taught to sell solutions.

Ten percent of salespeople will "get it" on their own. Thirty percent will never become solutions sellers because they cannot or will not. But 60 percent can learn to sell solutions and will, if trained. What you need to know, as a sales manager, is what training is needed and where to get it.

Training Needs
1–Prospect selection by profile. Solution sellers do not canvass tall buildings or industrial parks to find people who'll buy from them. Your salesperson must learn to select prospects who are likely to need

products or services we can deliver. The profile may be based on type of industry, size of company, title of buyer or specific applications.

2—Gaining access and establishing credibility with prospects. Access to C-level buyers, with bigger responsibilities, needs and budgets, is limited and must be earned. Credibility is the foot in the door. The seller's experience, research and approach signal to the C-level buyer that he/she is being approached by someone who can help, not by a product-pusher.

3—Ability to uncover needs and opportunities. Solutions sellers know which questions to ask and how to ask them to discover the priorities, needs and desires of top executives. The wrong question can end a meeting in less than a minute. The right questions, asked correctly, can lead to a profitable, long-term relationship.

4—How to move a sale through the cycle from prospect selection through multiple steps. This is accomplished in multiple meetings with various individuals or groups, discovering bumps or blocks in the road and effectively getting past them to the point of offering a solution, gaining permission to proceed and making delivery.

5—How to assure customer success and explore future opportunities. Solution sellers know that their job is to ensure not only that they have delivered what they produced, but also that the results they promised to the customer become reality. In doing that, they create the opening to explore future opportunities with the customer and those in his/her circle of influence.

You and your sales reps can learn to sell solutions. Here are some of the best resources accessible to everyone. Has your salesperson read them? Have you?

- *Consultative Selling*, Mack Hanan, AMACOM
- *Selling To VITO*, Anthony Parinello, Adams Media
- *The New Solution Selling*, Keith Eades, McGraw-Hill
- *Selling to Big Companies*, Jill Konrath, Dearborn
- *The SPIN Selling Fieldbook*, Neil Rackham, McGraw-Hill
- *Think Like Your Customer,* Bill Stinnett, McGraw-Hill

Seminars and training presented by manufacturers, vendors or industry groups and by companies like Sales Performance International and Huthwaite, Inc. are additional avenues of learning.

There is a ten-percent chance that you have a solution seller or a salesperson who can and will learn it on his/her own, sooner or later.

Sixty percent of salespeople can and will learn to sell solutions, if training is provided.

Hiring a solution seller is faster than training your current salesperson. However, you'll pay more and wait longer for sales results than if you hire the average raw recruit or a salesperson trained and experienced in your field.

Consider your business situation, your market and the odds. The choice is yours.

Developing Your Sales Team

I attended a program featuring inspirational writer and speaker Og Mandino, author of *The Greatest Salesman in the World* and 18 other books.

When introduced, he strode to the center of the platform and quietly made this statement: "You are who you are and you are where you are because of two things—the books you've read and the people you've met. One year from now, you will be exactly the same person in the same place you are tonight except for two things—the books you'll read and the people you'll meet." The rest of his speech implored the audience to upgrade the quality of their knowledge and acquaintances, thus upgrading the quality of their lives in the next 12 months.

If you are one of the many small business owners who make up the outside sales force for your company, may I ask what you plan to do this year to get better at selling?

If you are the sales manager for one, two or more full-time salespeople representing your business, what will you do this year to help your salespeople get better?

Here are 12 activities or tactics you may use with your salespeople to help them improve themselves and their sales:

- **January**—Buy a copy of *The Greatest Salesman in the World* for yourself and your salesperson(s). It is available at any bookstore and at Amazon.com for

$7 or less. Read it, or get the audio and listen to it. Assign it and discuss it. It may change your life.
Category: Books you read

- **February**—Arrange a conference call with an award winning sales person you know, yourself and your sales person(s). Prepare questions in advance, and be sure your salesperson takes notes on the call. If you don't know a top producer, look for their pictures and stories in newsletters or on conference programs.
Category: People you meet

- **March**—Get a copy of *The Little Red Book Of Selling* by Jeffrey Gitomer for yourself and each salesperson. It is $19.95 or less, everywhere. Assign specific chapters—they're short—that each of you will read and discuss each week.
Category: Books you read

- **April**—Send your salesperson(s) to a sales training program offered by your professional association, Chamber of Commerce, community college or by one of your suppliers. If possible, go with them. Meet the experts and hear what they have to say. Later, debrief the session and identify action items.
Category: People you meet

- **May**—Assign to yourself and each salesperson the reading of the current issue of your professional or trade magazine, cover to cover. Personnel, finance, management, sales, marketing—all of it. Discuss it in your sales meetings.
Category: Books you read

- **June**—Invite the best salesperson in your city to lunch with you and your salesperson(s)—maybe it's the top salesperson of one of your customers, a

vendor or someone else whom you respect. Ask him/her to share their story, sales philosophy, specific skills and tactics with you. Later, discuss what you learned.
Category: People you meet

- **July**—Buy two books. For yourself, *Superstar Sales Manager's Secrets;* for your salesperson, *Superstar Sales Secrets,* both by Barry Farber. You'll find each for $12.99 or less. Have your salesperson give a report on his/her book.
Category: Books you read

- **August**—Do a YouTube search for a video by an outstanding sales trainer such as Jeffrey Gitomer, Barry Farber, Brian Tracy, Zig Ziglar, Tom Hopkins or Jill Konrath. Make it the focus of a sales meeting. Watch the video and discuss how it applies to your specific selling situations.
Category: People you meet

- **September**—Buy everyone a copy of a sales classic such as *How I Raised Myself From Failure To Success In Selling* by Frank Bettger, *How To Sell Your Way Through Life* by Napoleon Hill or *The Psychology Of Selling* by Brian Tracy. Assign chapters to be discussed in weekly meetings.
Category: Books you read

- **October**— Arrange a conference call with an award winning sales person you know, yourself and your sales person(s). Prepare questions in advance, and be sure your salesperson takes notes on the call. If you don't know a top producer, look for their pictures and stories in newsletters or on conference programs.
Category: People you meet

November—Assign *Selling 2.0* by Josh Gordon or *Giants of Sales* by Tom Sant. Get the book for yourself and for each salesperson, under $12 everywhere. Have salespeople report on assignments and discuss what they learned.
Category: Books you read

- **December**—Invite another prominent salesperson in your city to lunch with you and your salesperson(s). Ask him/her to share their story, sales philosophy, specific skills and tactics with you. Later, discuss what you learned.
Category: People you meet

If you follow this plan, and your sales staff will be among the most knowledgeable, best prepared in your market. Will that make a difference in your business?

If you do not intentionally read books and meet people, who will you be and where will you be in the coming years?

"My sales are down 14 percent from this time last year. We've got to get them up. Can you work with my sales guy and help him get us more sales?" It's a call I get frequently from small business owners.

"I'll try. How are his sales for the year?" I asked.
"He's up about 17 percent," the owner responded.
I asked, "And what had you hoped for?"
"At least 15 percent."
"Well, friend," I offered, "it seems your salesperson has surpassed his goal. He's up 17 percent, yet your revenues are down 14 percent. Perhaps we should look somewhere else for the shortfall!"

I have had this conversation with a number of small business owners. That's understandable. Times are tough, money is tight, owners and managers have cut expenses and everyone needs more sales. We can offer suggestions to help salespeople increase their sales, but that may not be your problem.

We have discovered in a number of recent reviews that, even though the salesperson's sales were up by as much as 30 percent, company sales were flat or down a few percentage points. What's the problem? Usually, it is one of two things.

1—Customers are coming in the front door and going out the back. Regardless of business cycles, this is always a danger. A first time customer discovers you, through outside sales or your other marketing methods, and places a significant order, but doesn't return. Perhaps there was a problem, perhaps not.

Have you looked over your previous year's records to see how many significant one-time sales you had? Not one-time $100, jobs, but sizeable orders from first-time customers who haven't come back. Do the research, find out who they are and make someone responsible for contacting them, winning them back and developing their account.

2—Your base of house accounts is eroding. A successful salesperson maintains contact with customers based on a scale of relative worth. In our sales training, we recommend that a salesperson be in touch with "A" accounts at least once a week, "B" accounts every two to four weeks and "C" accounts every four to six weeks. "A" accounts are the salesperson's largest, most profitable ones, usually the top 20 or 25; "B"s, customers 26 through 50; and "C"s, 51 through 80 or so.

Some customer attrition will happen due to things you cannot control: moves, mergers, closings. Most likely, if your salesperson's sales are up but the company's sales are down, it's because your house accounts are being wooed away by the competition. Who, at your organization, is responsible for maintaining regular contact with them? You, the owner? A customer service rep? No one?

Someone must be responsible for touching your top customers on a weekly basis. If you are not doing this, start now. It costs five times more to acquire a new customer than to keep a current one happy. Surveys prove that the number one reason customers go away is that they feel taken for granted.

Remember, your top customers are your competitors' top prospects, so it is important to super-serve them.

Of course, you want your salesperson to sell more. But if his/her sales are up while yours are down, you need to figure out why and decide what you'll do about it.

Sales Management With Dr. Phil

We have defined solution selling as *an offering, made up of different components, which is proposed to resolve some specific issue(s) that a customer or prospect is experiencing.*

To be successful now and in the future, your sales rep must be able to reach upper level executives who have the authority to change business processes. The seller must be able to talk the clients' language, establish credibility and enter into a consulting relationship with them.

Does your salesperson have the skills to sell this way? If not, how will your business adopt this new way of selling? Either your salesperson must learn these skills or you need to hire one who has them. The only other choice is to continue with a rep who is using yesterday's methods to sell the same products at lower prices, tighter margins, against more competition.

Solution selling requires a new way to manage your "new" salesperson. I call it The Dr. Phil Method.

Whether faced with an individual who can't control his behavior or a couple who can't communicate, Dr. Phil always asks the same questions. These are the ones your solution seller will ask of prospects and the ones you should employ as a sales manager. Just imagine you are Dr. Phil, without the television show, several best-selling books and millions of dollars.

The four types of questions are:

- **CONDITION** questions are asked to determine the current situation.

  Dr. Phil asks, "What's going on in your home?" Or, "What are you trying to accomplish in your career?"

  Your solution seller will ask a prospect, "What are you trying to accomplish this quarter/this year?" Or, "How is your company adapting to the changes in the industry?"

  You will ask your sales rep, "What are you doing to reach three new decision-makers this week?" Or, "How do you plan to hit your target for new business proposals this month?"

- **PROBLEM** questions seek to learn what issues may be keeping the subject from accomplishing the objective.

  Dr. Phil asks this question the same way every time: "Well, how's that working for you?"

  Your rep will ask, "What are you doing to hit your target?" Or, "Are there issues that threaten its achievement?"

  Wearing your sales manager hat, you will ask questions such as, "Were you able to get a meeting with Prospect A for this week? Or, "Is networking alone going to get you there?"

- **IMPACT** questions are designed to link an individual's or department's problems to others, dramatizing the need to address the problem.

  Dr. Phil asks, "So how are your temper tantrums affecting your kids?" Or, "Does that mean you put in more hours at work, rather than go home?" He'll follow up with 'what then' questions like, "What happens then? Are the kids afraid of you? Are they acting up at school? Do you think this makes them feel insecure about how Mom and Dad get along?" You get the picture.

  Your solution seller will ask, "So, if the company doesn't achieve the 26 percent sales growth target, what does that mean to you? To your boss? To her boss? To the CFO? To the shareholders?"

  You'll ask your sales rep, "If you don't get these three meetings this week, what does that mean for next month?" or "If we don't get to at least do a demo, why would they move over here?" Then, "What will that mean to your new business goal? Then what happens? What will happen after that?"

- **PAYOFF** questions ask what if? And they seek to determine the value of working together.

  Here's Dr. Phil: "If you could find a better way to deal with the little hassles, would that keep you from blowing up?" Or, "Would you like it if Mom and Dad weren't always on your back about the friends you choose? What if you made better choices? What would happen then? And would that help with your grades?"

Your salesperson: "If we could find a way to get a better conversion rate on your leads, would that be of value? If we could double it, what would that mean to you, your boss, the company? Would that bring value to you?"

Sales manager: "If you could get one more appointment a day, would that catch you up by the end of the year?" or "What if we could get them to call you and ask for an appointment, instead? Is that worth looking at?"

We ask questions to learn what's going on today, how it is breaking down or could work better, how that would affect people in other areas and then to create the vision of a better future if we work together.

When Dr. Phil helps someone get their life under control, he's a hero. When Sara helps a customer find a better way to reach their customers, she creates value. When you help your sales rep reach her goal, it benefits her and you.

The Sales Prevention Department

Gil Cargill is a Los Angeles based trainer who says that many companies look to skills training as a solution to a problem that has nothing to do with salespeople's selling skills.

He says that, instead of fixating on a single skill or skill set that needs improvement, sales organizations will view training as a panacea to address a host of problems he refers to as the Sales Prevention Department.

"The Sales Prevention Department is a conglomeration of haphazard, inaccurate, sloppy administration, billing, manufacturing, delivery, shipping and customer support issues. So when those functions fail, the customer calls the sales reps, who are then rendered incapable of selling the next deal because they are too busy patching up the last one. The problem is looking to sales training to fix issues that have nothing to do with a salesperson's skills!"

Inaccurate billing, production errors, incomplete orders delivered to the wrong location and indifferent customer service are just the start of the symptoms of a Sales Prevention Department. What are some others?

• **No coordinated marketing program**. If you do not have a consistent direct marketing program to your prospects and customers, you are engaged in sales prevention. If you do not have a current (qualified within the past six months) prospect and customer list, you're doing sales prevention.

Direct mail creates a "warm call" environment for your salesperson's calls and visits. Paid search advertising, your website, email, social media, mobile, local radio and television are all part of a coordinated marketing program.

Does your sales rep know which postcard you mailed last month to the people he's calling on now? Put him/her on the mailing list so they know and can reinforce that message on their next call.

Point: Don't place all of the blame for unsatisfactory sales on your salesperson if you aren't supporting his/her activities with a coordinated marketing program. Sending the salesperson to a seminar or having her call an expert won't fix that.

• **Wasted sales leads**. Many companies – perhaps yours, too – put a lot of time, money and energy into trade shows, local advertising, signage and décor to get prospects to raise their hands and say, "I might be interested in buying from you."

What happens next? If it takes more than 24 hours to get a quote to a customer or prospect, your front end is the Sales Prevention Department. If the request is a sizeable one from a first-timer and you do not personally follow-up on it or assign it to a CSR or salesperson for follow-up, that's sales prevention.

Point: Sales training will not fix failure to follow-up on leads.

• **Failure to provide sales skills training**. Putting Sales Representative or Account Manager on an untrained employee's business card does not impart selling skills to him/her. They won't get needed skills by breathing the air in the office. Sending them out into the world with notepads but no knowledge is sales prevention.

Salespeople are not born. People learn how to sell. Books, audio and video programs, webinars, websites, local and national seminars, manufacturer training materials, local college or continuing education courses in selling, vendor resources – all are available for instruction in selling skills.

• Point: Do not place the blame for lack of results on someone for whom no training was provided.

You may think of several other items that could fit under the Sales Prevention Department, things like incompetence, rude and unprofessional behavior by any staff member or focusing on what we produce rather than what customers want and need. And as the leader of your business, you must always be thinking and looking for ways to remove obstacles to profitable growth.

Key to Your Success: An Outside Sales Effort

For a few years you've been hearing about how solution selling is the next way to build your business and secure its future. That's because buyers and buying processes have changed. In the old days, salespeople had all the knowledge. If a buyer had a problem, he'd talk with a salesperson about it. The salesperson would share as much information as it took to make the sale and the buyer would get something close to what he wanted.

It's different now. Buyers have as much or more information at their fingertips than the salesperson do. Not only can they go to the manufacturer's web page and find what they think they want, get the specs and pricing, they can also read reviews of people who have bought the gadget. If the reviews aren't good, the buyer will go on to the next one.

Sales is no longer going out and offering what you have to buyers. It is about going out to buyers to find out what their needs and challenges are and finding a solution for them – even if your company doesn't make or service it. "What we sell" is not as important as what the customer wants or needs.

Why this emphasis? There are several reasons:

1—Times are tough.
2—Revenues are down.
3—Cash is tight.
4—Competitors and clients are failing.
5—You have fewer people and there's no money for new equipment purchases.

6—You have excess capacity, product sitting in warehouses, costing you money. And so do your prospects.

In order to grow sales, increase profits, differentiate ourselves from our competitors and ensure our long-term success, we have to get out and tell the story.

- **Value-added services must be sold.** The key to success is that someone must go to customers and have a conversation about what they need to achieve. It begins by asking what they have and how its working for them, then shifts to what they need to have and what it needs to do for them. The difference between what they have and what they need or want is your opportunity.

  Customers don't care what you can do. They only care about what you can do for them and how you can help them accomplish their business objectives.
  Your outside salesperson will be the point person to do the inquiry with your prospects and customers. You may also wish to designate yourself or a key employee to take the message to your best house accounts.

- **Start with existing customers.** The reasons are obvious: you already have a relationship with them, you know their businesses, they trust you and will be anxious to learn about a new service that can help them. Once you have some customer success stories, you can use them to go after prospects for new business.

- **What's the payoff to your business?** First, you will keep your best customers. You will screen out competitors from getting in by offering something new that the customer doesn't know you do.

  Second, you will sell more to your best customers. You've proved this over and over. When you added new products, services, sizes, colors, bundles or packaging, your best customers bought those, too. It will happen again. You'll make more money.

  Third, you'll gain new customers. When you have some success stories, you'll call on prospects to discuss solutions to problems, not competitive bids on one-time projects.

When your customer decides to put that huge parts manual on the Internet, what will you do to replace that business? The time to think about value-added services has past. Now it is time to commit to it, choose one new service, get educated and start selling it. Someone has to sell it. If you don't have an outside salesperson, now is the time to get one on the street.

Part Three

Managing A Salesperson

Goals Drive Sales Performance

Success in any venture is driven by the goals set for it. That is why business books, sales seminars and consultants talk so much about goals. Goals are mileposts along the way, to ensure that the individual or organization attains its purpose.

Why did you hire your current salesperson(s)? Most likely, to help your company attain its purpose, as defined by you. How do you know whether they are doing that?

The correct answer is by setting standards of performance, targets or goals, and measuring the rep's progress by the goals that were set. But too many times, the answer is, "I'm not sure." You tell me that your salesperson is seeing a lot of people, picking up a lot of leads and having a lot of appointments; he's doing a lot of proposals, but the money's not coming in like you think it should. You're not getting the results you expected.

Then, when I inquire about your expectations, the answer I usually get is "Well, we never really set specific numbers. I showed him a chart of first-year sales and said that was average, but we didn't really make it law."

So, if I understand you correctly, you're telling me that your salesperson isn't hitting an undefined target. Correct?

How do you know he isn't hitting it? How does he know he isn't hitting it if he was never given the goal?

Would you expect an archer to be able to hit anywhere on the target if there wasn't one? Or if it was hidden behind a drape?

Would you want your doctor to perform surgery on you without a goal in mind? What if he just wanted to peek inside and see what's what?

I consider myself to be a pretty good scratch photographer. I don't have a fancy camera or the knowledge to operate one. I use a simple auto-focus digital camera with no changeable lenses or special lighting equipment. But I don't just point and shoot.

Whether I am in New Orleans, one of my favorite cities for taking pictures, eating and enjoying music, or on a cruise ship in Alaska, my goal is to have a good time and get some "pretty good" photos. As long as I'm not trying to make a living by getting shots for *National Geographic,* pretty good is good enough for me. But if I was taking pictures while blindfolded or with the lens cap on, I could not even be pretty good.

I encourage you to write this down and put it someplace where you'll see it often: *If your salesperson is not working to reach your goals, he is working to reach his own—and that may not be in the best interest of your business!*

Your rep's goal may be to do as few cold calls as he can possibly get away with. Her goal may be to do just enough to be pretty good and to keep from getting fired. But your goal is for the salesperson to get to break-even as quickly as possible, increase your firm's sales and make money for the shareholders. In the process, she will make a good living, too.

But are those goals? No. Those are wishes that may never become reality.

Salespeople will work toward goals. The key is for you and the salesperson to set performance goals together, write them down, refer to them often and use them to manage the rep for top performance.

The sales effort should be measured in two ways: activities (cold calls, phone calls, appointments, demos, quotes) and revenue. Revenue is the result of activities. If your rep does a sufficient number of the right activities with the right prospects and customers, the desired revenue will result. But, if she does not engage in the right activities with the right people, consistently and well, the results will be disappointing.

So the real key to sales success is to set goals for activities and revenue and to manage to those goals. It is easier to do so from week one than to restart after months of lackluster sales, so be sure to get started right.

Priorities for Sales Management

If I asked you to tell me your number one priority as a business owner, you'd probably say, "Depends on what day it is." Right? One day your top priority is solving a customer's problem, another day it is working on equipment, personnel or accounting issues. All of these are priorities, but you can only focus on one at a time.

Similarly, if I ask, "What is your number one priority as the sales manager for your business?" Your answer might be, "Depends on the day." Right again.

There are five priorities for sales managers: recruiting, hiring, training, managing and coaching, the five section headings in this book.

- **Recruiting** is an ongoing, never-ending activity for a sales manager. Wherever you are and whatever you're doing, always be on the lookout for someone who might make a good sales rep. It involves working your network of customers, suppliers, peers, neighbors and friends, looking for an exceptional candidate – even when you don't need to hire someone. In planning for future growth and in managing your business day to day, be aware of who is out there and who might make a great contribution to your team.

- **Hiring** is also a priority. The sales manager, possibly the small business owner, engages in hiring only one salesperson at a time and, one hopes, not too frequently. Hiring is more an event than an ongoing activity, but it is the process of choosing a candidate, selling him/her on the opportunity and negotiating an employment agreement. Hiring is expensive in time and money, and mistakes are costly. It is important to make the best hire for any position.

- **Training** begins with the hiring interview, I believe, as you share with the candidate the specifics of the job: time, place, activities, goal setting, measurement, review process and the rest. Training continues as long as the individual is in your employ.

- **Managing** salespeople well is key to their development and your satisfaction with them. A common definition of sales management is, "accomplishing the revenue goals of the organization through your sales representatives." Planning, directing, monitoring, fine-tuning, measuring and redefining are components of effective sales management.

- **Coaching** involves teaching, training, correcting, motivating, recognizing and challenging salespeople. It includes the most personally demanding activities in sales management. As coach, you need to get inside each salesperson's head to know what makes him/her perform. Is it praise, recognition, money or something else? Then, using your skills as a salesperson/business owner/parent/manager/psychiatrist/fortune teller—did I leave anything out?—you lead the salesperson to perform at a higher level.

So, which is more important? It depends on the day, and on you and your salesperson(s). Focus on your priorities and work on today's number-one objective while looking ahead to what you'll need next.

The Triangle of Sales Success

Is your salesperson a "10"?

In an ideal world, we'd all have all 10's, but the odds are against it. The fact is that in any sales organization, 20% of salespeople will be top performers, 20% will be poor performers and 60% will be average. It is one thing to deal with those percentages when you run an operation with dozens or hundreds of salespeople. It is quite another when you have one salesperson or two, as many small businesses do.

Unlike a mammoth insurance company, you cannot hire a thousand salespeople, knowing that half of them will wash out in a few months and you will end up with 80 or so top performers from the remainder. You must be more selective in hiring, more thorough in training and be quicker to cut your losses when you find you've hired a "2" instead of a "10."

What makes the difference? Two specific traits differentiate super-achievers from the under-achievers.

First, in most cases, the top salespeople have been selling for their current employer for a number of years. We call this "time in service."

Second, the top people have a higher level of selling skills than the others.

If you have done formal study in sales management, somewhere along the line you have come across the Triangle of Sales Success.

One of the equal sides is **knowledge**. Top sales reps are thoroughly familiar with their product/service, their market, their customers and their competitors. As the owner/sales manager, you are responsible for providing them with resources to become knowledgeable in these areas. Of course, the salesperson must want to learn; you can't make him. A salesperson who can't or won't learn your business will not help you or himself. Top salespeople will look for opportunities to increase their knowledge to remain successful.

The second side of the triangle is **professional skills.** These are the skills of prospecting, qualifying, setting appointments, making presentations, closing and follow-up. No one was born knowing how to do these things; they must learn them. If your salesperson is weak in one or more of these areas, it is up to you to point them toward the training they need to acquire these skills. Books, CD and DVD programs, online videos, classes, seminars—all teach those skills. If your salesperson will not apply himself/herself to improving his skills, he will remain an average performer, at best.

The third equal side of the triangle is **motivation**, the will to win, the ability to bounce back after rejection/disappointment and the daily commitment to a positive attitude regarding the future. Motivation comes from within. A sales manager can cajole, drive, threaten or inspire, but cannot motivate a salesperson. If he doesn't have "it" you can't inject "it." You need to demonstrate your own drive, energy, will to win, bounce-back-ability and positive attitude because salespeople take their cues from the manager.

Do you have a 10? Then celebrate that by taking good care of your salesperson! But realize that by building his/her knowledge, professional skills and motivation, a 4 can become a 6, maybe a 7 in time, and build a solid book of profitable business for you.

There is no such thing as a born salesperson. Successful salespeople are men and women who have prepared themselves with the knowledge and professional skills needed to succeed and who have the inner drive to be the best they can be.

Your challenge is to develop successful salespeople.

Who Else Wants A Root Canal?

Fall and football bring with them the task of business planning for the coming year. Business planning is like having a root canal – nobody wants to do it, it is painful and unpleasant and it is put off as long as possible. Once it is done, though, the pain goes away, you feel better and you're proud of yourself for having done it. You may wonder why you didn't do it before.

But not yet.

Business plans come in all shapes and sizes. Herb Kelleher started Southwest Airlines with a business plan sketched on a cocktail napkin. Yale student Fred Smith's business plan for FedEx started out as a college class assignment.

Whether you write out a one-minute business plan, a business plan lite or a full-blown one, your chances for accomplishing the things you wish to do in the future are greatly enhanced when you have a written plan. And more so when you manage your business by your plan.

That is true, of course, of the sales planning that goes into your larger business plan. If you have salespeople, you may ask them to write their sales plans for inclusion. If you are your salesperson, the task is up to you.

At its simplest, the sales plan answers these three questions:

Where am I now?
Where do I want to go?
How will I get there?

The Sales Planning Tools to use:
• A Product Opportunity Planner, a dashboard view of your top 25 accounts, which allows you to see what gaps to fill with products and services.

• A People Opportunity Planner, like the Product Activity Planner except that it focuses on people within the organization.

• An Account Strategy Plan to complete for each of your top 25 accounts, beginning with the current people and products and calling for specific steps to target specific prospects in those accounts, so you can grow those accounts. The same type of plan is used to target prospects and how you will convert them into customers.

John Aiello is CEO of a sales consulting firm based in Chicago. In an article on sales enablement, he wrote: "Within a sales organization, managers can measure an infinite number of factors when trying to gauge success. At the end of the day, however, there are only five that matter and sales enablement directly impacts each one."

The metrics that most directly impact revenue attainment are:
1. Number of opportunities in the pipeline
2. Average deal size
3. Win rate

4. Length of the sales cycle
5. Total number of active (or "fully ramped")
salespeople

Each of these metrics should be addressed in your
sales plan. How many prospects/customers shall you
target? What size prospect is ideal for you? How much
more do you need to get from an existing customer?
What is the likelihood that you'll do that, and how
soon? Finally, who will help you accomplish that? Do
you have the sales staff to attain that growth, or will
you need to hire?

Having a great sales plan won't make you successful;
but consistently implementing even a good one will
make a positive difference in your business.

Plan Now for Sales Growth

There are two ways to get to the top of an oak tree. You can climb it or sit on an acorn. – H. Frank Brown

There are two ways to improve your sales this year. You can plan for it, or hope for it. One of my all-time favorite book titles is *Hope Is Not A Strategy* by Rich Page. Results are more predictable with a plan, so you need to have one.

In creating your sales plan, there are several components to evaluate, including:

- Current sales
- Potential growth in existing accounts
- Potential loss of existing accounts
- Potential conversion of A and B prospects to customer status
- Your referral development strategy
- Activity count (number of cold calls, telemarketing calls, appointments, referrals)
- Your professional development

Current Sales
Start with a printout from your financial program, showing year-to-date sales for your top 50 accounts, then project 12-month sales from them for this year.

Potential Growth in Existing Accounts
Your best source for increased sales is current customers. Based upon your knowledge of them and their industries, conversations with them and the local business outlook, estimate their possible buying increase for the next year. What additional products and

services will you sell to them? Consider what each company is buying from you and who the buyers are, as well as what they are not buying from you and who additional buyers might be. Assign a dollar increase to each one and figure the percentage increase.

Potential Loss of Existing Accounts
Many businesses lose 10 to 15 percent of your customers each year, through no fault of their own. Companies move, get bought out or close. Your goal is always to be sure you lose the right ones, not the top ones. Consider whom you may lose to factors like those, and some whom you may decide to release.

Potential Conversion of A and B Prospects
Which of your best prospects seem to be moving toward becoming customers? If you've been actively working your prospects, you should be able to make an educated guess as to which ones will convert within the next month, quarter, year and how much that business will be worth to you. Determine the activities you will perform to move them onto the customer list: direct mail, phone calls, e-mail marketing, key prospect marketing, open house, special events and others.

Referral Development Strategy
Eighty percent of prospects who come to you by referral are likely to become customers, whereas only 20 percent of those resulting from cold calls will ever convert. It is important that you develop a strategy for getting internal and external referrals from existing customers. That begins with asking your best, most profitable, most satisfied customers for testimonials and introductions to others within their company whom you might serve. Then, ask for referrals to their contacts in professional groups and associations.

Activity Count

At what level will you perform the activities that lead to sales increases? Be specific in setting targets for the number of cold calls, telemarketing calls, appointments, mailings, estimates, demos, etc. Which of these activities can you delegate and which of your other activities can you delegate, to make time for selling?

Professional Development

To maintain their licenses, your doctor, lawyer, broker, realtor, insurance agent, pilot and others must take a certain number of hours of continuing education each year. That helps them to stay current with advances in their fields and competent to provide the best service to you, the patient or customer.

What have you done this year to improve your knowledge of selling, of your industry and of your company's growing capabilities? Get specific regarding the number of trade magazines and books you'll read, the number of audio or video webinars you will take, the courses you will take, the seminars you will attend. If you make it part of your plan, it is much more likely to get done. Don't your customers deserve a better salesperson next year? Don't you owe it to yourself and to your family to be better than you are right now?

As a business owner, you have many responsibilities, including planning for sales growth. Set aside time to create your sales plan, and then do it.

Writing Your Sales Plan

When we approach the fourth quarter of the year, it's time to take stock of how we've done during the current year and plan for the year to come. A part of your business plan is planning for sales growth.

Companies with employed outside salespeople should consider involving them in the business planning process. Doing so could range from having each rep write a sales plan to doing a joint exercise with them and incorporating that into the company's business plan. Regardless of who is writing the sales plan, there are several elements that should be included:

- **Current customer sales.** Print out your year-to-date sales report. It will be apparent that about 80 percent of your business comes from 20 percent of your customers. These are the key customers going forward. Have the sales of this group grown this year? Have one or two of the big customers cut way back this year? Do you expect that to continue, or is a rebound coming? Has their business changed? How will that affect you? How to know? Talk with them. In planning for next year, write down the number you can reasonably expect to see from each one, based on past performance. Add or subtract to get a realistic number.

- **Current customer sales growth.** If you anticipate growth in this group based on new buyers, more invoices or larger invoices, figure that into your plan for next year. Write the number down as either a dollar or percentage figure, by customer. Then consider what you will do or have done to create that growth. Have you added capabilities or new products to your line this year? Have you increased your marketing activities such as telemarketing and/or direct mail? Did you add a salesperson? Will you be adding additional products or services?

- **Potential new sales from qualified prospects.** Print out or write down your top 25 qualified prospects. A qualified prospect is one who has the real or perceived need for what you sell, as well as the money and authority to buy it and who has shown some interest in buying from you. You have current contact names and, perhaps, have even met with them, but they have not been converted into customers yet. Put down what you can conservatively expect in sales from each one. Add that number in.

- **Activities.** As you did with current customer sales growth, write down the activities you must do to generate that sales growth. Will you add services or staff? Will you increase mailings from 12 to 15, or from once a month to twice a month? Will you do more marketing activities or some local advertising? Will you join a networking group? Get more referrals? How will you create sales from people who are not yet your customers?

- **Niches.** Will you target specific niches? Which job functions/titles will you target: marketing, human resources, sales? The more specific you are regarding industry niches, particular companies or organizations, departments or job functions, the more likely you are to make your plan work.

Simply stated, your sales plan for the year is made up of your sales in the previous year plus anticipated growth/loss in those accounts plus anticipated new customer sales and the tactics you will employ to get them.

The sales plan becomes part of your overall marketing plan, which helps you to write your business plan for the coming year.

Mining Your Most Valuable Asset

Look around your business and think about the most valuable thing you own. If you woke up tomorrow and your building was gone, or all of its contents had been destroyed by a hurricane, you could survive if you still had that one thing. Most business owners know it is their customer list.

I know you. You are among the most creative, resourceful people on earth. If someone walks in with a job you don't know how to do, you figure it out. You can get the work done, here, there or somewhere. But what you cannot live without is customers.

Your customer list is the most precious asset of your business. Here are some other things you know:
  • Selling more to existing customers is easier than always having to find new ones.
  • Selling to existing customers is less expensive than constantly finding new ones.
  • Selling to existing customers creates more predictable income, known margins and cash flow.

Your Best Prospect For New Products or Services
You don't need another prospect list to sell new offerings. Your best prospects are your current customers for whom you now provide some of their product. They are the owners and marketing executives at the companies on your customer list, but you're working for a software buyer or an IT or procurement admin.

Rather than try to get an appointment with a stranger and try to talk him into a "blizzit program," you or your salesperson should be asking for an introduction to the marketing manager in your client company. They know you. They like you. You're in the system. They send you business now. They pay you for your work now. You don't have to get on The Vendor List. Then, go have a conversation with that marketing manager, but remember this: it is not his job to buy blizzits, that is not what he wants to talk about and if you talk about blizzits, he will send you back to the person who buys it from you.

Your best prospect is the person at your client company who is responsible for growing sales, customer acquisition and retention, cross-selling and up-selling current customers, expanding and protecting the brand. Why go after anyone else?

Sure, a salesperson must always be doing new business acquisition activities because stuff happens – companies move, close, get bought out, etc. You have to replace 10-15 percent of your customers every year. But your best, easiest, quickest chance for profitable sales growth is to sell more to existing customers.

In sales planning sessions I have reps do an exercise where they list top customers, contacts and the products and services they sell to them. The next step is to find opportunities in those companies – people who do not buy from us, people who buy hard goods from us but have never purchased our soft goods. Without exception, those who do that exercise are surprised at what they learn.

One small business owner put her palm to her forehead and exclaimed, "Dumb! Dumb! Dumb!" When asked why, she said, "I just figured out I left $250,000 on the table this year because of what my best customers are not buying from me!"

Peter Drucker did the research and said that:
- Your chances of making a sale to a new prospect are **1 in 14.**
- Your chances of making a sale to someone who's not currently a customer, but has bought from you in the past, are **1 in 4.**
- Your chances of making a sale to a current customer are **1 in 2.**

To sell more, be sure your salesperson is asking. Ask your regular contacts who is responsible for growing the business, for customer loyalty and for managing the brand. That is your ideal prospect. Ask to be introduced to the person responsible for employee/customer retention and ask that person for a meeting. Ask questions about how they do what they do, how its working or not, and whether they'd be open to an idea or two you might have to do that better. That will increase your value to them.

What About Sales Meetings?

A small business owner sent an e-mail saying, "I know we need to have sales meetings. What should one look like? What should happen? How often should I have one? How long should it be? What should I do or say?" Perhaps you're wondering the same thing, so let's talk about two types of sales meetings: daily and weekly.

Daily. It is crucial that you, the sales manager, spend some time every day talking with new salesperson(s). Especially in the early days, you want to have an informal chat every day, preferably one in the morning and one at the end of the day. This is just a "What are you going to do? What did you do?" kind of conversation. Its main purpose is to ensure that you spend some time with them.

Unless you set aside time to do this—even five minutes—other responsibilities may prevent you from speaking with them. If you fail to do this, your new hires will come up with their own reasons why you're not talking to them: you don't have time for them, you don't like them, you're questioning or regretting your hiring decision, they're not as important as others in the business, or that outside sales isn't really that important to you, after all.

Other questions to ask in these informal chats include: How many dials did you do? How many actual conversations? Whom did you talk to? Were they receptive? Did you get any appointments, orders, requests for estimates or proposals, etc.? What did they ask that you didn't have the answer for? How do you feel the day went? Are you feeling comfortable with the system?

We do these things to get an understanding of how the rep is feeling and what they're thinking, and to let them know they're an important part of our business and that they are doing valuable work.

We also do these things to catch unintentional mistakes early. For example, if he says he spent the morning making calls at the mall, this is a good time to correct that. If she has told several people on the phone that you don't offer overnight delivery, would you prefer to correct that today or in three weeks? Obviously, the sooner you address it, the better.

So, make the time to have a "How's it going?" chat with your salesperson every day.

Weekly. For a more formal weekly meeting, an agenda is in order. This type of meeting may be a half-hour or an hour long. After a few months it may become a semiweekly meeting. Whereas the daily meeting is one-on-one, the weekly meeting may include one or all of your salespeople.

Here is a sample agenda you may use.

1. **Ask what your rep is proud of.** "Tell me about the best call you had last/this week." Give your rep a chance to brag. We all like to do that.

2. **Review call reports**, commenting on specific notes, specific companies or contacts about which you may have some knowledge, such as, "We've been trying to get in there for two years," or, "The guy we used to do work for left there and we lost touch." Look for detail (too much? too little?) in CRM notes. Ask what he/she thinks the value of these notes is, and how

thorough they need to be. Regarding two or three promising prospects, ask, "What do we need to do next? What do you see as most important in our approaching them? How do we get further than the marketing assistant?" Talk about tactics, tools and the next call.

3. **Review activity goals and performance.** If they made only 72 percent of the calls they expected to make in a week, what's the problem? Are they spending too much time on each call, or too much time between calls? If they have goals for call-to-appointment ratios, how are they doing? What can you do to help them improve? Stress the need to get back on track and obtain their commitment to do so.

4. **Set one or two specific objectives for the coming week**, such as, "To get the answer to one more qualifying question than I usually get," or, "To average one more call per day." One objective might be to read an article from an industry publication and be prepared to talk about it next week.

5. **Ask the rep, "What do you need from me/us to do better in the next week?** Are there any internal obstacles that are keeping you from a better performance?"

6. **End the meeting with encouragement** such as, "I think this is going really well. I'm pleased with your work and your progress. Once you get this down, it's going to be a ton of fun and you're going to make some serious money." Or, "I know you're not completely comfortable with the system yet, but it's coming. I'd like to see you get better with the phone

scripts and I know you will. It takes some time, but the system works, we know that, and it's going to work for you, too."

7. **Set the time and place of the next meeting.** Communication between the salesperson(s) and the sales manager is crucial for the success of your outside sales efforts.

Five Things Your Salesperson Doesn't Want To Do

There are two kinds of people in the world: those who speak in broad generalizations and those who don't. I am going to speak in broad generalizations regarding five things most salespeople don't want to do. While I find these to be true of most salespeople, they don't apply to every one and, perhaps, not to yours—right now.

1—Your salesperson doesn't want to cold call. He/she finds cold calling fearsome, demeaning, ineffective or a waste of time. No salesperson looks forward to cold calling and most live for the day they can just service existing customers and rely on referrals for growth. There are seminars, books and tapes ranging from *The Complete Idiot's Guide to Cold Calling* to *Cold Calling for Cowards* and *I'd Rather Have a Root Canal Than Do Cold Calling.*

As sales manager, you must see that they do enough of it to keep their pipeline loaded. As a million-dollar seller told at a sales seminar, "You can never stop cold calling. I did, and it came back to bite me. Now, I'm out there doing it again."

Your salesperson doesn't want to cold call? No one does, but it is part of the job.

2—Your salesperson does not want to keep records and turn in reports. You aren't the only manager who has to badger them to get reports. Most salespeople are big-picture, broad-stroke, fast-paced doers, not reporters. They get commissioned on sales, not reports, so they may find record-keeping tedious or a waste of time.

A Top Performer once told me, "Man, I don't keep records of any kind. No computer notes, no paper lists. I know my customers and what they buy." I asked him, "What happens if you get run over by a bus?" He understood the risk and admitted that no one else could pick up the account and move forward with it.

It is crucial that you have sales records and get some level of reporting from your salespeople. It's your business! New salespeople need more oversight than proven performers, but what happens if...?

Your rep doesn't want to keep records and turn in reports? No one does, but it is part of the job.

3—Your salesperson doesn't want to lose a proposal. When a long-pursued prospect finally says, "Well, gimme a price on that," the salesperson wants to win. Most want to win the first job, no matter what the margin is, just to get the customer.

That first opportunity is probably going to be based on beating the price the prospect is paying now. What your salesperson knows is that he/she has done everything right so far, and finally has a chance with this prospect, and they want to complete the transaction. As the owner/manager, you want your salesperson to succeed, but you have to make a profit. Sometimes you stand firm on price; sometimes you bend. Explain why. You might ask if she'd participate in the discount by giving up some of her commission.

Your salesperson says your prices are too high and she could sell a lot more if you'd lower them? She is neither special nor unusual. They all say that.

4—Your salesperson doesn't want to lose a customer. That's why he's often back in the warehouse, shrink-wrapping and bothering people instead of out there selling. He has done everything right, from cold call to qualifying to getting an appointment, making a presentation, winning the quote and getting the job. Now he's afraid something will go wrong. He tells me, "For every one I bring in the front door, one goes out the back door because we messed up. It's hard to get ahead that way."

You need to have systems in place to keep errors to a minimum, especially on first-timers, but mistakes happen. When they do, your salesperson is likely to be no more understanding than the customer and you may hear, "Why can't they just get it right? Do I have to do everything myself?"

Your seller worries about losing a customer? They all do.

5—Your salesperson doesn't want to leave. He/she took this job with great expectations and visions of success: money, awards, prestige and personal satisfaction. They all do. She also expected to be educated, trained, managed and coached to success. With that kind of support and her hard work, your salesperson should succeed.

There are four reasons salespeople fail:

- They don't know what to do.
- They know what to do, but don't know how to do it.
- They know what to do and how to do it, but don't do it.
- They know what to do and how to do it, but don't want to do it.

As the sales manager, it is your job to provide training and motivation to your salesperson. It is the salesperson's job to accept and apply the training and do the work because they want to succeed. It takes more than desire from both. Your salesperson doesn't want to leave. She wants to hit all her targets and succeed. They all do.

Managing Solution Sellers

Let's begin by restating our definition of solution selling: an offering, made up of different components, which is proposed to resolve some specific issue(s) that a customer or prospect is experiencing.

For you, the owner or sales manager, selling solutions is not a new concept, even if it is a new term. Nearly twenty years ago, as a new business owner attending training offered by the franchisor, I was taught that the way to build our start-up business was to go out and make friends, then find out what they needed and get it for them, even if we didn't make it, stock it or ship it. You've been doing that for years.

So, selling solutions is not a departure from what you've been doing. It is, instead, the next step in delivering on the current message to customers and prospects in our marketing and advertising and in person: We will help *you* reach *your* prospects and customers more effectively.

Earlier, we discussed hiring and training a solution seller and the resources to help you do that. Now it is time to talk about managing the solution seller you grow or hire. What you will need to adjust is the type of expectations and measurements you have regarding prospecting, presenting and closing business.

As the business owner and/or sales manager, you have specific measurements that define success for a salesperson. First, you measure activities—telemarketing calls and appointments, then revenue. Unless a new sales rep is hitting the activity targets early, he/she probably will not hit the revenue targets that follow.

Unless you are extremely patient or paying no attention, you are still going to measure those things as your rep moves to selling solutions. But you will begin to measure other activities, as well. These include weekly and monthly metrics not expected to produce short-term orders for individual jobs or even projects, but high-level, long-term customers. You will set expectations for your rep to meet targets such as:

- **Doing more sophisticated, more focused prospecting via networking,** Internet research, use of association/industry directories and matching to a profile of the type of customers you need to develop. Beginning salespeople will still develop many of their prospects through old-fashioned and reliable door-knocking on cold calls, which are intended to discover suspects and, if they're lucky, some immediate or short-term jobs.
- **Focusing on identifying key upper-level individuals inside the prospect company**, and then on discovering their major goals and initiatives to see how you can help them accomplish the things on which they get measured.
- **Arranging meetings to interview those individuals, with specific questions to ask.**
- **Planning for the call** in which the salespersons will present your solution—read the definition again—as a package to help them meet their plan to increase revenue, cut costs, retain customers, gain market share, etc.
- **Planning and arranging follow-up meetings** as necessary, or removal from the prospect list.

- If successful, going deeper and wider into the organization to capture the full potential of the business.

Sound like what you and your salesperson have been doing all along? Great! You just need a structure to measure its success.

Sound like a foreign language? That's okay. You can learn it.

Why Salespeople Quit – And What We Can Do About It

Most of the salespeople who leave their employment are not fired; they quit. There are some common reasons for their resignations.

1—They don't know what to do. First-time salespeople do not know what to do. They must be taught about your business and be taught how to sell, and both must begin on day one. Product knowledge can be taught by owners and others in the company, by vendors, by books and DVDs and seminars. Some business owners can teach selling skills by example, from their own experience, or by using materials provided by the company and outside sources. Whatever the source and however training is delivered, it must be delivered. Salespeople who do not know what to do will either do nothing or will do a lot of things wrong. In both cases, they will produce negative results and will quit or be terminated. We must train them.

2—They know what to do, but don't want to do it. Having taken a job where rewards are based upon performance, and having been trained to do the work, some new reps decide they don't want this job, after all. After being on the job for about a month, one salesman attended a sales seminar only to go home and quit his job the next week. Did he just want a free trip to California? Maybe. Or, maybe, he learned that this job was going to be harder than he thought, and he didn't wan to do it. You must be clear about expectations when the salesperson is hired, and he/she must be held to those expectations. If they don't want to fail, they'll either do the work or quit.

3—They get discouraged. Selling is hard work, especially during the first few months. Sales reps get many more rejections and stalls than orders, and it is easier to admit defeat and quit than it is to fight through the tough times. You need to encourage them to keep putting in the effort, which, if done consistently, will produce positive results. An old expression says, "Even a blind squirrel will find a nut, eventually." If the manager provides positive support early, perhaps the salesperson will not quit out of discouragement.

4—They take another job, just like estimators and drivers and other key employees do. Whether it is because of low wages, no benefits and little respect, or because of the lure of easier or more important work, more money or greater opportunity for advancement, people are going to move on. Salespeople, too. What can we do about it? Practically, nothing.

There are dozens of other reasons for quitting, such as: I was tired of being nagged; I hate being micro-managed; they wouldn't pay me commissions I was owed; the owner didn't trust me; the shop was a failure factory; we weren't a good match for each other; I'm going back to school; I can't work under those conditions, etc. The bottom line seems to be unmet expectations.

Ideally, you will provide the kind of environment where the salesperson can reach his goals while helping you reach yours.

The Key Is Consistency

I am fortunate to own a magnificent old clock that has been in my family since the late 1800s. It made the trip with my father's father's family when they moved from Alabama to Texas around 1900, and it has been in our home for about 20 years. It was working when it was passed to me, but the wooden case was a mess. I engaged a craftsman to clean it up and bring out its beauty.

It is an 8-day kitchen clock that winds with a key and chimes on the hour. Actually, it clangs on the hour, a decidedly non-melodious tone, like a kid banging on a pan with a wooden spoon. But I like it.

This beautiful, hand-built timekeeping instrument isn't particularly good at keeping time. When it is fully wound, it runs fast, so it is always ahead of the "real" time. As it winds down, it runs slower, so it is always behind. It is somewhat reliable during about three days of the week, days three, four and five. The rest of the time, it is either fast or slow. Of the entire eight days it runs on one winding, this clock is precisely correct for just a few hours on day four, so I am always comparing it with "real" time.

But this treasured family heirloom has been entrusted to me, and I have come to appreciate its clanging and its approximate measure of time.

What does this have to do with sales and sales management?

Very likely, your firm's sales effort and my clock are alike in their inconsistency. When sales slow, you don't notice it at first. As time goes by, you begin to notice the drop-off, and then what do you do? Wind up your sales program! You begin to make thank-you or check-up calls to customers, you drop in to see them, you mail some postcards, you start paying more attention to what your salesperson does all day.

And what happens? Sales pick up. You see more jobs coming in, billings go up and you have a month or two when sales are good, certainly ahead of the slow month.

Then what happens? Sales activities drop off, because you're so busy trying to get work out the door that you don't take the time to wind up your selling activities.

What about your salesperson? As his energy and sales begin to slow, a sales clinic comes along. He goes, picks up some new ideas, gets inspired by being around other salespeople and gets refocused on selling. Like that clock when freshly wound, he displays renewed energy and commitment to building business. He makes more visits, more calls, asks for referrals, goes on appointments, closes more business and clangs more often. Good news!

Then the salesperson gets so busy servicing accounts, checking on projects, delivering jobs and following up on estimates that he/she doesn't have time to make the calls and visits and other sales activities that build business. So sales wind down, and you both get frustrated. Then a sales meeting comes along, and the cycle begins again.

Does it sometimes seem to you that your sales program is only "right" about 20 percent of the time? And if you've been in this business for 10 or 20 or 30 years, you know it's always been that way.

So, the key to success is consistent effort, with sales activities and with clock winding.

I can tell when my clock is running fast—it clangs faster! When the clanging slows down, it's time to wind it up again, lest the clock and clang stop.

You know when your sales are running ahead, and if you pay close attention, you can tell when they begin to slow. Most sales reps give off clues as to attitude, energy and motivation. When they begin to slow, that is the time to encourage and challenge them. Reward their successes and help them learn from their losses. Challenge them to go higher and deeper into client companies, to ask for referrals and testimonials, to learn more about document services and their applications.

My clock doesn't run on a quartz crystal, synchronized with the U.S. Naval Observatory master clock, but I don't need that. I just need to avoid the extremes. So do you, your salesperson and your outside sales program.

Rewarding Superior Performance

Question: My salesperson has just had a spectacular sales month, greatly exceeding his goal and setting a new personal sales record. I'd like to do something special for him. What do you suggest?

Answer: There are many ways to reward and recognize a salesperson—or any employee, for that matter—who has performed beyond expectations. Depending upon the type and scope of the achievement, and on how well you know the individual and his/her family, hobbies, etc., you may choose to give a reward that is work-related or one that is purely personal. Here are several examples in each category. For more ideas, pick up *1001 Ways to Reward Employees* by Bob Nelson ($10.95) at local bookstores or from amazon.com.

Work Related
- Certificate of Outstanding Performance, presented at a meeting of the entire staff
- Plaque, presented at a staff meeting
- Letter to the customers of the salesperson, recognizing the achievement
- Newsletter profile, including photo and personal information
- Paid parking, if not usually provided
- Monthly pass for bus or subway, if appropriate
- Upgraded sample kit
- Calculator
- Book
- Smart phone
- Gift card

Personal/Family-Related

- Cash
- Flowers
- Time off
- Tuition for a class or course
- One month's car payment
- One month's maid service
- Babysitter for a special occasion
- Handyman service for a home project
- Item for personal collection
- Sports equipment
- Prepaid phone card
- Autographed items
- Dinner with significant other
- Tickets to ballgame or concert
- Gift certificate for food, fun, photo session with family, golf, cooking school, day spa, car washes, seminars, interior design, fruit-of-the-month, flower-of-the-month, beer-of-the-month, book-of-the-month
- Gift certificate from giftcertificates.com that may be used at a number of merchants, including Omaha Steaks™, Saks™ and Sephora™.

To make the reward special, make it personal.

Salesperson's Image Gets New Emphasis

In the current competitive business environment, business owners have evaluated every facet of their operations and have made changes to become more efficient and more effective. Most likely, owners and sales managers have taken a similar approach to the outside sales efforts. Perhaps you have added a salesperson or two, added outside telemarketing, purchased a new prospect list, joined a new networking or leads group, upgraded computers and/or software, reassigned accounts, or otherwise made changes to your sales operations.

It is time to take a good look at your salesperson(s).

In a *Sales & Marketing Management* magazine survey of 360 executives, 30 percent say that customers have commented negatively on a rep's appearance or grooming. And 49 percent say their salespeople have encountered prejudice from customers because of the way they look. 48 percent say salespeople's physical image has become more important.

In the same survey, S&MM asked, "What type of sales rep has a tougher time making sales?" The top five responses shouldn't surprise you:

- A salesperson with body odor (72%)
- One who uses profanity (61%)
- One who smokes heavily in front of clients (61%)
- One who drinks heavily in front of clients (52%)
- A sloppily dressed salesperson (48%)

The magazine goes on to say that other factors such as the salesperson's proper dining manners, greeting etiquette (introductions, handshake) and the nuances of body language and eye contact contribute to a stranger's positive or negative impression of the salesperson.

What do you think? Have you lost business because of a salesperson's negative appearance or behavior? 38 percent of those surveyed believe their company has. If you think your salesperson is turning prospects off, she probably is.

If you want to find out, ask a few of her customers, "How are things going with (Amy)? Are you happy with her service? Does she get back to you promptly? Does she solve problems for you? Is there anything she does that irritates you? What do you think of her appearance? What could she do to serve you better?" You'll get answers.

If your salesperson looks good, conducts herself well, has good manners and happy customers, tell her how important that is, and how much you appreciate her attention to those details.

What if there's a problem? Is it grooming, clothes, manners, body language (or body odor), bad breath? As the manager, you need to bring it to your salesperson's attention and ask her to do better. That is a touchy thing to do. It may offend her. She may throw a fit. She might even quit! So, carefully consider what you will say, how you will say it, where you will say it, even whether you are the right person to say it.

Here's a start. Be sure your salesperson reads this article. You might discuss it in a sales meeting. Don't you talk with them about keeping the office neat and clean? Approach it from the point that "we always want to be sure that we're creating positive impressions on others." If she doesn't take the hint, you'll have to be more direct.

(Note to salespeople: If you're reading this, it doesn't mean your manager hates the way you look or act! Read it anyway, and then go ask someone who'll be honest with you.)

There's help. If manner of dress or grooming is the issue, refer your salesperson to one of these resources:

- *The New Professional Image* by Susan Bixler and Nancy Nix-Rice
- *Professional Presence* by Susan Bixler
- *Casual Power: How to Power Up Your Nonverbal Communication and Dress Down for Success* by Sherry Maysonave
- *You Are What You Wear* by William Thourlby

In addition, there are millions of links to "image consultants" on the internet.

Does your salesperson need to wear a power suit and power tie? Not necessarily. If one calls on downtown lawyers or corporate headquarters, you'll be better received if you look like them. If you call on customers in office/warehouse parks, you should be more casual.

The best advice is the old advice to dress one level above your customer's. These days, it may be more important than before.

Who's Got The Monkey?

Good morning, Sales Manager. Time to do some sales coaching – like you have nothing else to do as the business owner, vice-president of human resources, tax collector and compliance officer for the city/county/state/federal government, facilities manager, estimator, billing department, collection agent, customer service/complaint department, temporary employee of the day in whichever department someone doesn't show up, delivery driver and the one who goes to Sam's Club on Saturday to restock paper towels and bathroom tissue at the shop.

I know who you are and you're out of paper towels, too.

You walk in this morning with half a dozen monkeys on your back – issues, challenges, concerns, priorities and tasks – that you must deal with. During the course of the day, you'll move one monkey off your back and onto the admin's: "Toni, call the copier tech and tell him its doing that thing again." Later you'll transfer a monkey to the delivery guy, "Jack, when you deliver to Fawcet, be sure the invoice gets to Heather over there."

You'll also take on some new monkeys, as your staff members, customers and vendors come to you with, "Where's the... Did you call... The network's down again... I need off Wednesday," etc.

And then your favorite person, your sales rep will come into your office, plop down in the chair, gently take the monkey from her back and place it on yours with, "Can

Donner have 130 personalized golf towels for their tournament Thursday?"

What you do in the next 30 seconds determines where that monkey perches for the next two hours: on your back, the sales rep's back, a CSR's back, a vendor's back or a competitor's.

Who's got the monkey?

If you say, "Let me look at their production schedule in the catalog," the monkey is your back. If you say, "Call John at Trinkets & Things," it is handed back to the sales rep, who'll pass it on. Say, "Ask Anna to go on the website and see what they say," the sales admin gets the monkey. Say, "Can't be done," and the monkey goes elsewhere.

You're doing it right when everyone has monkeys appropriate to his/her function in the business. That keeps the monkeys healthy, fed and cared for. But your reality may be that you, the owner/manager, are bowed over under the weight of everyone's monkeys, doing what someone else could do, while they are standing in line, outside your door, with nothing to do.

How to handle the monkeys? Instead of saying, "Let me give that some thought and get back to you," or, "I'll take care of that as soon as I finish this," put the monkey where it belongs. Perhaps these questions will help.
> What do you feel you need?
> Why is that so important to you?
> What ideas do you have to resolve the situation?
> How do you think you'll accomplish this?
> Have you tried...?

Did you look...?
Is there another way to get the same result?
If you did have a solution, what would it look
   like?
Who knows more about this than you?
Where could you go to find a solution?
See if you can come up with an idea to prevent
   this next time.

There are monkeys only you can handle. If this is not one of them, assign it to the best person to care for it, and carry on with your own.

The title and the inspiration for this chapter came from William Oncken, Jr. and Donald Wass, who published an article on this topic in the Harvard Business Review twenty-five years ago. Their premise was that a manager has multiple demands on his/her time and it is crucial that one learns to manage the monkeys.

You might profit from *The One Minute Manager Meets The Monkey* by Kenneth Blanchard, William Oncken Jr. and Hal Burrows, published in 1991. It is available in bookstores, real and virtual.

Back in the good old days, customers were loyal. As long as we met their needs, treated them fairly, expressed our appreciation for their business and did their work right, we were rewarded by their loyalty. They bought from us because of our relationship, built on trust and service.

It is no secret that things have changed. We still do what we've always done, but we don't always get the same results. We have some customers who will always be loyal, but not nearly as many as we'd like or as we'd like to think we have.

When the economy turns bad, many of our customers find themselves under the same kind of money pressures as we fall under. Like us, customers cut expenses to maintain some profit and survive. One place they find to cut is procurement. They cut back, order less often, order smaller quantities, move some things to the Internet. Some move all their business to an offshore parts dealer with lower prices.

What can we do today to safeguard our customers in the months and years ahead? I think it begins with asking yourself and your salesperson(s) some serious questions, including:

How difficult is it for my customer to switch suppliers? You know that what sometimes kept a prospect from switching to our company is that the other provider had all the plans, artwork, field guides or whatever. Today the question is, who is helping our company succeed? If you've established yourself as a business partner providing solutions from conception to archival, how likely is your customer to leave you for someone who offers less, to save a penny a gross?

What would my customer lose if he changed suppliers? What do you offer—products, people or procedures—that your customer could not find elsewhere? "Quality and service" is not a good answer because the fact is that most people in your business offer an acceptable level of quality and service. Would he lose special pricing, document storage and fulfillment? Your online ordering system ties the customer to you. If a customer has bought into the need for this service, bought the system, trained his employees to use it, set up his customers for online ordering through it, he would forfeit all that if he went away. And if you've helped him develop an integrated marketing program that gets the results he needs to grow his business, all of that would be lost. What would your customer lose if he changed suppliers?

Do I maintain regular contact with my customers? Frequent contact keeps small problems from becoming big problems. It also strengthens relationships. Integrated marketing activities: phone calls, e-mails, postcards, newsletters, personal visits—they all count. Never forget that your top 20 customers are someone else's top 20 prospects, and if your competitor is better at contacting your customers than you are, you run a real risk of losing them.

Do my customer and I have a long-term commitment to each other? Here is another area where selling products versus selling solutions is a wide gulf. When you go beyond asking what jobs she'll be sending over this week to asking what her strategic initiatives are for this year, you go from being a typical salesperson to being a business consultant. When you go from talking about the number of color pages in the manual to how to increase her response rate and generate more revenue, you move toward cementing a relationship that will be more difficult for a competitor to violate.

Can I document what I've done for my customer lately? Can your customer document for her boss or her board why she's doing business with you? If she called and asked for documentation, could you provide it, in terms of meeting deadlines, improving processes, reducing costs, increasing income? Most buyers don't have time to do that on every vendor they're buying from. Do they know what you're doing to save or make them money?

Think through these questions with your top 20 customers in mind. Discuss them with your salesperson(s). Strategize on strengthening your customer relationships and finding ways to bond with them for the future.

Managing in Difficult Times

Things never stay the same. They get better or they get worse but you don't often hear anyone say that things are like they've always been. They're not. Things are not even like they were yesterday, and tomorrow they will be different.

You and your clients deal with a constantly changing marketplace. You gain new clients and lose others, buyers change jobs, companies change the way they do business.

As a business owner, sometimes salesperson and, most likely, sales manager, you must keep four truths in mind and instill them in your sales team:

1—Someone, somewhere, somehow will sell something, and it might as well be you. Someone set new all-time records last year, in a market just like yours, and it will happen again this year. Who are those people? How did they do it? How do they plan to set new highs this year? Why? Why not you? How can you do that?

2—Your strategies have to be more accurate than ever. You must be in front of the right people at the right time with the right message. That's the meaning of relevancy. The message must be clear and concise.

3—Changing times require that you and your team work smarter. You already work hard. You need to work smarter. Selecting your niche, refining your approach, prioritizing your time and energy to the things that matter most, that give you the greatest return on investment—these things require more thinking and planning.

4—There is no such thing as down time. You can't afford to think of slow times as down time you really needed so you could get your filing in order, paint the lobby or take some time off. When business is rocking you can rest a bit, but when times are slow, that is no time to slack off. It's true that one has to make hay while the sun shines, but if the barn is empty and there is hay to be made, one may have to put lights on the harvester and bale after dark.

Until all is well in your world, there are specific actions the sales manager must employ to help the sales rep achieve his goals and contribute to the success of the business.

First, hold the salesperson accountable. We all perform better when we know someone's watching. If you have included your salesperson in business planning and goal setting, as you should have, he should know that you are holding him responsible for carrying his share of the load. Help him understand that it is not okay to not hit the target and that, while stuff happens, it is important to get back on track quickly.

Second, measure activity. That's how you know whether your salesperson is on track. Sales activities, performed consistently and competently to the right prospects and customers, are credible predictors of sales results. If your salesperson is engaged in smart prospecting, qualifying, presenting, closing and servicing, she will produce results. If they are less than expected, she must do more or do better to produce greater results. Sales success and failure are predictable.

Third, keep the pressure on. Hang the charts, color the graphs, write names on the white board to remind your salesperson that he has made commitments and you're counting on him to meet them. Neither you nor the rep should be surprised at the numbers at the end of the month or quarter. Make the goal clear; make clear that the goal is a commitment you expect him to fulfill.

Finally, stay positive. Your positive attitude and communication may be the biggest carrot you have to coax your salesperson to outstanding achievement. There is a world of difference between a manager saying, "What's the matter with you, Mark? You know what I expect, and if you don't get busy and produce, we're going to have a serious problem, mister!" and, "Mark, I know you're working hard, and I'm as disappointed as you about the lack of results from your efforts. I am confident you can do this. What do you think you need to do differently?"

Keeping yourself positive and focused on sales growth is the best way to keep your salesperson positive and focused on sales growth. You are on the same team.

Part Four

Coaching A Salesperson

Hey, Mister, What Kind of Dog Do You Have There?

A few years ago, Blair Singer and Robert Kiyosaki wrote *Sales Dogs: You Do Not Have to Be an Attack Dog to Be Successful in Sales* by. In it, they described five types of salespeople and identified them with breeds of dogs with common traits. As you read these brief descriptions, see if you can determine which kind of sales dog you have and what it means to you and your business.

The Golden Retriever. They'll do anything for anyone willing to pet them. They will jump into freezing rivers after rotten sticks, play center field for your son's softball team, maybe even bring you a beer from the refrigerator.

This is the eternally optimistic salesperson with a big smile who wins clients by racing after anything that the prospect throws to them. They will fetch any ball, do any favor and bend over backwards to please the prospect. To the Retriever, customer service is everything. Long-term service is the key.

The Poodle is highly intelligent and high-strung. These salespeople tend to have flash and class: sharp suits, buffed out shoes or stiletto pumps, and cool cars. But they don't consider clothes, cars and jewelry to be luxury items. They are simply tools of the Poodle trade.

The Poodles probably have extensive networks. They love to be the center of attention. Their sales pitch is delivered with such style and panache that even the ones without a shred of logic sound visionary! They are the Ultimate Marketing Dog, and they can make a lot of money.

The Pit Bull. The most aggressive salesperson is the Pit Bull. They attack with a ferocity, aggression and tenacity that is both awe-inspiring and terrifying. All they need is a pant cuff to latch onto and they NEVER let go. They are absolutely fearless. Handling objections and closing are what they love most.

The Pit Bull's success comes from shear power and fearlessness. They will make more calls, field more rejections and keep on selling more than any other breed—even when they should really back off. Adversity is simply a wake-up call.

The Chihuahua is a technical wizard with amazing brainpower. Their product knowledge and understanding of processes is astounding. They are insistent about driving their point home, and their constant high-pitched "yipping" may give everyone else a headache.

While others are curled up asleep, the Chihuahua is flitting from website to website, or page after page of annual reports, assembling a report that would take others twice the time.

The Bassett Hound is hard to resist. This companion will stick by you through thick and thin. You may try to chase this dog away; yet, it would always come back. Bassetts are never ruffled, never stressed; they are consistent and dependable.

When they sell, they have that distinctively humble approach that goes right to the heart.   Their pathetic look and begging—or even pictures of the family—may be employed to get sympathy. They are incredible tracking and hunting dogs whose tenacity is rivaled only by the Pit Bull. Their favorite word is "please" as in, "Please give me this order."

So, which one is your salesperson? Each one has its strengths and can be successful. Each one also has its shortcomings and traits that must be trained to have less effect in their behavior.

How does one coach a Chihuahua to success? What are the shortcomings of the Golden Retriever and what must the salesperson do to compensate for them? It's all in the book. Get a copy for yourself and your salesperson. See if you can agree on which breed your rep is. Identify strengths and weaknesses, and let the book suggest ways to make up for shortcomings. Some people will not buy from a flashy Poodle; some will want your Pit Bull put to sleep! Talk about what it all means to your salesperson's career and to your business.

The Sales Dogs™ website is www.salesdogs.com.

What Every Salesperson Needs

Here's good news: there is no such thing as a natural born sales manager. Every successful sales manager learned to do it, and so can you.

There are four things every salesperson needs from his/her manager. Every business owner has the ability to provide at least one of them, with no training. And every one can learn to provide all of them by using the tools and assistance available to every owner. Here they are:

1—Every salesperson needs knowledge: of the company, your product, your customers, your industry and your competition. You have this knowledge and the ability to transfer it over time, not overnight, to a sales representative. You also have the responsibility for doing that. If your salesperson does not know your company, product, customer, industry and competition, it is not her fault.

2—Every salesperson needs selling skills. There is no such thing as a natural born salesman. Most likely, your new salesperson has never been in your industry and has never sold anything. Selling skills must be learned. Among the things to look for in a sales prospect are aptitude and a willingness to learn.

What are the six selling skills they must learn?
Prospecting
Qualifying
Getting appointments
Presenting
Closing
Follow-up

Unless you offer skills training and the employee learns them, she will fail. If you were fortunate enough to land an experienced sales rep, provide opportunities to upgrade her skills.

3—Every salesperson needs direction and focus.
Even an experienced salesperson needs to be directed to the right types of products and services to sell to the right market, and a sales rookie doesn't have a clue. You do! You know your business and your market area, who the customers and best prospects are. They don't. You must direct them and keep their activities focused on reaching the right people with the right products and services.

If your salesperson is underperforming and wandering aimlessly through the territory, bringing in nothing but thermo business card orders, don't blame her. Point your rep toward the right people and maintain that focus.

4—Every salesperson needs motivation. Hire positive people who exhibit enthusiasm, confidence, persistence, discipline and positive thinking. Check references and have staff members interview them to confirm your impressions. Hire happy, can-do people, and then provide an environment that won't sap their inner motivation. Be sure they can feed off your own enthusiasm and positive expectations. In time, your salesperson will become the top revenue generator for your company—in essence, your number one customer. Expect much of her and take care of her as you would your best customer.

What Motivates a Salesperson

What keeps a salesperson going? What makes him/her get out of bed every day, knowing there will be more noes than yeses, more rejections than acceptances? What keeps a top performing rep going? I have asked top sellers and here's what they told me.

- **Family.** The number one motivator for these super sellers was their family. They work hard to be successful so they can provide for their families, and improve their circumstances. They want their families to be proud of them.

- **Money and what it can buy.** For some, it is the commission check that drives them to perform, but most said it is what the money buys – houses, cars, pools, braces, private schools, fishing vacations, financial security, etc.

- **Recognition.** Some top salespeople crave recognition, from sales awards to plaques and even pats on the back. For some, being praised in front of the rest of the staff is reason enough to get up and do it again tomorrow. Others just need to know the boss recognizes how hard they work and what they contribute to the company.

- **Challenge.** Top performers love the challenge of solving problems, whether helping with a customer's need or finding the hot button that converts a highly desired prospect into a customer.

- **Desire to win/desire to succeed.** High achievers strive to be the best because they have the desire for it. This is the inner drive, the "fire in the belly" that cannot be implanted into any person, including a salesperson. They have it or they don't. We can't teach it and it cannot be learned. Most high achievers have it.

- **Fear.** Even for some who are super successful at selling, fear remains a top motivator. Some fear that if they let up for a day, they'll lose their edge. Or maybe their house. Fear of falling behind, being number two or missing out on opportunities drives them to keep pushing.

What does this mean to you, the sales manager?

First, it means that you should not presume to know what is the main motivator for your sales rep. Do what we did: ask him or her, and consider the answer when determining in-house sales contest prizes or bonuses.

If family is your rep's hot button, challenge him with a bonus or prize the family can enjoy: passes to a movie, concert or ball game, a trip or a home theater system.

If money is it, set up compensation tiers. For example, offer an additional commission percentage point for exceeding the monthly or quarterly sales goal, and another one for every multiple over that.

Recognition may be as simple as making a Salesperson of the Quarter award, even if you only have one salesperson and she qualifies for it every quarter. Certificates, plaques, additional training opportunities, all will work. She also wants private recognition. Make specific praise and thanks part of your management.

If you have a large enough sales staff, use competition to challenge your reps. Form teams to compete against each other in short-term contests: cold calling, appointments, presentations, demonstrations, tours of your operation, etc. Set challenging goals together, and work to accomplish them.

Fear works best as a self-management tactic, rather than an imposed one. There is a time and place, though, for leveling with a poor performer whom you have decided you need to help move up or move out. Presenting a rep with specific activities, numbers and results, which must be met within 60 days or else, may create pressure to perform. It may also encourage him to look for other work, which may be fine with you by now.

Of course, motivation is personal with every member of your creative and production teams as well. To get your people to perform at their best, find out what's important to them and offer them a way to get it.

How To Motivate Your Salesperson

"How can I motivate my salesperson?"
"How do I get her to sell more?"
"What can I do to help him? I don't know anything about selling!"

I do not believe one person can motivate another. I believe, instead, that motivation comes from within. One person can inspire another. Inspiration from without often motivates me to do something faster, better, more efficiently or in a more detailed manner, provide better follow-up, etc.

Listen to some of the experts on how to motivate, challenge or inspire your salesperson or sales team to greater performance.

"Smart sales managers recognize that achievement and recognition of achievement are the two most powerful motivators in sales. So instead of cracking the whip, they are whipping up contests, games, spiffs, and awards that keep their sales professionals focused, happy, and engaged." – Jeb Blount, author of *Power Principles*

"I believe that in the long run, salespeople are responsible for motivating themselves. However, there is most definitely such a thing as a de-motivator. The manager's role is to support and reinforce the efforts of a motivated person. Without realizing it, a manager can sap the motivation right out of his salespeople. A manager can de-motivate them by creating a stressful, negative work environment." – Landy Chase, speaker and writer on professional selling and sales management

"In tough times, sellers must be at the top of their game. As a sales manager, your job is to infuse your team with fresh thinking – to make sure they have the knowledge and skills to deal with today's challenges. Start a "book of the month" club. Register for webinars or teleseminars put on by sales experts. Encourage sign up for sales e-newsletters. Lead weekly "how we won" sessions." – Jill Konrath, author of *Selling to Big Companies*

"To create momentum, keep your sales team focused on what they need to do today, or this week, by implementing a 20 point system. On this system, they earn points for doing the right types of sales activities: conversations, appointments booked, face-to-face meetings, referrals, closed files and closed business. The focus on the right kind of activities with targeted prospects will result in creating the desired energy." – Danita Bye, President of Sales Growth Specialists

"Salespeople will be excited to come to work when they adopt a referral-selling strategy. They'll meet with decision makers, shorten their sales process, and convert prospects to clients more than 50% of the time—while acing out the competition and landing new, profitable clients. They'll meet only with the people they want to meet and who want to meet them. What an irresistible proposition! Money in their pockets. What a great motivator!" – Joanne Black, author of *No More Cold Calling*

"Sales managers should hold a meeting with their sales teams with a focus on creating two lists: one containing the things the salespeople CAN'T control, and one containing the things they CAN control. Managers should then encourage their salespeople to focus 100% of their attention on the things they CAN control. Nothing blows away feelings of helplessness like having an action plan and TAKING DAILY ACTION against that plan." – Alan Rigg, author of *"How to Beat the 80/20 Rule in Sales Team Performance"*

Inspire your salespersons. Recognize them. Don't be a de-motivator. Focus on activities, not personalities. Train, educate and encourage them. Provide a fertile field in which inspiration, creativity, activity, victory and celebration can thrive.

Conducting a Customer Audit

It is a good idea to sit down with your salesperson(s) on a regular basis, perhaps during your monthly sales meeting, and ask some questions to keep them focused on customer retention and growth. Start with each salesperson's top five accounts. Have them do an audit on each customer and buying patterns. Ask the salesperson to compile the following information and report to you at the next meeting.

1—How many buyers do we have at the company?

One sales manager said of his top salesperson, "She's very good at penetrating new accounts, but she doesn't work as hard on trying to find more than one buyer in the company." That is not uncommon. Why don't reps work harder at finding additional buyers? Perhaps the "thrill of the hunt" has been satisfied. Or he wants to wait until the relationship is better established before asking for referrals to others. Or, maybe, he simply does not think to ask who else buys things like the client he has.

2—What are their titles and in what departments do they work?

An old lion-tamer said, "If you can't name 'em, you can't tame 'em." If you don't know the cats well enough to call them by name, you cannot know how to coax them to do what you want them to do. If your salesperson does not know the titles and departments of buyers, she is not ready or able to produce additional business from the company. If she does know that the sales manager at an auto dealership is the one who orders the blow-ups of newspaper ads to hang in the showroom, she may guess that other sales managers at other dealerships might be interested in having their ads enlarged, too. In addition, if she is only getting work from sales managers, perhaps she should be talking to the service managers too.

3—What have they ordered from us in the past six months? Have the salesperson do an audit of every item the buyer has ordered. Both of you may be either dismayed or pleasantly surprised at the breadth of services the company is using.

4—What have they not ordered in the past six months, or ever? The rep may be so happy to get that order for 10,000 soft poly covers every two months that he never thinks to ask what goes in them, and what goes with that. He may find that, up until six months ago, a customer ordered 30 units every two weeks, but hasn't done it since then. What happened? Unless one sits down and writes out what the customer is doing, such a change could go unnoticed until it is too late. The reason may be as simple as a new person doing the ordering.

5—What have we never asked them to buy?

Maybe the reason the customer has never ordered a common item from you is that she doesn't know you offer it. It has happened before, hasn't it? Customers forget, buyers come and go, salespeople change. If your sales rep cannot remember offering a specific item to a customer, it is time to ask for that business. And, unless your salesperson is completely current on your value-added services, there is a 100 percent chance that she has never asked her top five customers about other products you make or could provide. Would you like to learn that next week or six months from now?

By focusing on the salesperson's top accounts to see who is buying what and how buying patterns may have changed, you may discover gaps that your company can fill by simply asking for new, different or additional business. For the next meeting, ask for the audit on customers six through 10. Then, do the same audit on your house accounts, or assign it to a staff member. It is the easiest and quickest way to increase sales.

Sales Success—It's All in the Numbers

In his book *The 100 Absolutely Unbreakable Laws of Business Success,* Brian Tracy states Law #59 as the Law of Sales: Nothing happens until a sale takes place.

You already know that. You don't write an order, buy the wheelies, assemble the cart, deliver, or print an invoice until somebody sells something. And, of course, a sale is never really complete until the customer's check clears the bank!

Tracy also has these five corollaries of the Law of Sales, which are important for you to reinforce with your salesperson(s):

Corollary #1—Products and services are sold, not bought. No matter how good the product or service is, someone has to sell it. Selling is a process that involves finding prospects, determining their needs and ability to buy, discovering their specific need regarding your product or service and presenting your offering as the only reasonable, logical choice for that prospect.

#2—Customers need to be asked to buy. The job of the salesperson is to help the customer through indecision or hesitation to the point of placing an order. The failure to ask for the business is the reason most sales never happen.

#3—80% of sales are closed after the fifth call or after the fifth closing attempt. It is not expected that someone will buy from your salesperson on the first, second, third, fourth or fifth call. That would be the exception. Many salespeople get discouraged and give up on a prospect too soon. Be sure yours has a variety of contacts (in person, phone, mail, e-mail) to keep progressing toward the sale.

#4—50% of salespeople quit after the first call in a complex sale, and 50% fail to ask for the order even once in a simple sale. If your salesperson is asking for the business only four times, he is giving up too soon. If your rep has a qualified prospect—defined as one who has the need and the money to buy what you sell and who is open to buying it from you—be sure he sticks with the process.

#5—Ask and you shall receive. Becoming a top salesperson is not a miracle. Top salespeople see more people and ask more often.

Tracy says, "One of my clients, a billion-dollar company in California, paid thousands of dollars to an outside consulting firm to find out why its sales were down. (The consultants) found that...the average salesperson was making only four customer contacts per week.

"Based on these findings, and with no other changes, the company immediately instituted a contact management system that required each salesperson to meet, face-to-face, with at least two prospects per day, ten prospects per week. Companywide sales jumped 50 percent in the following month and continued to rise thereafter. This proved again that no amount of training or skill can replace the need to get face-to-face with prospects and customers."

In your next meeting, remind your sales rep(s) of the 80% and 50% rules and that the way to be more successful is to see more people and ask for their business more often.

The most successful salespeople are those who have better answers because they ask better questions. That is a matter of experience, training and practice.

We teach new salespeople to ask simple questions such as "Who buys this? How often? How many? From whom? Who else?" They elicit simple answers, which lead to fairly simple sales, and simple sales are quicker sales. That's what you and your new salesperson want! Those are also smaller sales. Remember your first? Was it a rubber stamp? 50 greeting cards? A keyboard? Weren't you thrilled?

But as salespeople gain experience and learn to ask better questions, they can move up in the organization to help buyers on a higher level solve bigger problems. Brian Tracy says, "Your compensation will be in direct proportion to the size of the problems you solve." Reps learn to ask, "Who does that? Why? How is it working for you? What if...? Would it help you to...?" And as they practice the art of asking bigger questions, they are able to provide larger solutions and make larger sales.

As sales manager, you should have reasonable expectations about what your salesperson is capable of producing, and then clearly communicate those expectations. Provide training, motivation and recognition as your salesperson grows.

The call came from a manager whose salesperson had hit the wall. This top achiever's sales had been stagnant for the two years. The question was, "What's wrong? Why aren't his sales growing? What should I do?"

The first answer was, "Be glad sales have been steady the past two years. Many companies and salespeople have seen declining sales." But that did not address the larger question: what DO you do when your salesperson seems to have topped out?

First, some DON'Ts.

- **DON'T cut compensation or divide territory** in hopes that you will push him/her to sell more. It is de-motivating. Those were common methods of motivation for higher sales in the days when beatings were administered to improve morale. In this third millennium A.D., that does not work. Salespeople have choices, and most often they choose to leave. Only attempt to restructure compensation or territories midstream when you don't care whether the salesperson stays or goes.

- **DON'T threaten the rep's job**. A "perform or we'll find someone who will" threat will also send a salesperson on job interviews. Don't use a heavy-handed threat on a salesperson you wish to keep.

What should you do when your salesperson has flat lined?

- **DO look for reasons why**, starting with the obvious ones: changes in the overall economy or in your local market. Are companies closing, downsizing or leaving your area? Have there been major changes within your company, such as the departure of key production personnel?

  Then consider personal issues such as illness or an accident, bereavement, family or personal crises, legal problems, etc. Are you still at a loss? Ask your salesperson what he sees as the reason(s) sales are not increasing. In some cases you will find one or two major factors. In others, there will be several smaller issues.

- **DO review current accounts**. With your salesperson, conduct an analysis of his accounts as to trends in dollar volume, number, size and frequency of orders and types of products purchased. As you do so, opportunities for additional sales may leap out at you. Focus your salesperson on:
  1. *Selling new products.* Identify two or three products a customer has never purchased from you, but could and should. Of course, if you have acquired new equipment or capabilities a customer has never used, it might be because she doesn't know about them.
  2. *Looking for additional buyers in the company.* If only the marketing people are ordering from you, your rep should target human resources, administration and other departments.

- **DO review time and territory management**. Is too much of your salesperson's time and effort being expended upon low or lower-volume customers? At what threshold should someone else in the office be made responsible for servicing customers, freeing time for the salesperson to pursue higher volume accounts? Is he spending too much time in the office, doing production or administrative tasks during selling hours? Are appointments and visits scheduled so as to minimize travel time?

- **DO set challenging goals with your sales representative.** Have both of you become comfortable with the current level of performance? A major motivator for sellers is having reachable but challenging goals. Once they are established, agree on the activities necessary to reach them, and then hold the salesperson accountable.

Like business owners, salespeople reach a comfort level with a good base of business, long-time customers they enjoy and a routine that is more account management than selling. For some, setting new meaningful goals will offer new motivation to build sales. Others decide to maintain their sales level and work just hard enough to find new customers to replace those lost each year to attrition. As manager, your next move is, most likely, to add a new salesperson to your staff.

What Every Salesperson Wants For The New Year – Any New Year

A few years ago, consultant Debra Thompson published a list of the ten things employees want in the workplace, #1 being the most important down to #10, the least important.

1—Interesting work
2—Appreciation and recognition
3—Feeling "in" on things
4—Job security
5—Good wages
6—Promotion and growth in the organization
7—Good working conditions
8—Personal loyalty to employees
9—Tactful discipline
10—Sympathetic help with personal problems.

Your salesperson, like all of your other employees, has a list that looks something like this one. But there are some other things your sales rep has on his/her wish list again this year. I know this. They tell me. As Tony Montana said in the movie Scarface, "I have ears. I hear things." Here are six things that every salesperson wants:

1–Your time and attention. In many small to medium sized companies, the salesperson is the "lone ranger," having no one with whom she can swap stories and share ideas. They need you to show your commitment and interest in the critical work they do, with your time and attention. Your salesperson works in an adversarial environment. Out there, on the street, she faces indifference, rejection and numerous obstacles, from gatekeepers to approved vendor lists and Three Quote Monty. In here, she faces busy production schedules, conflicting priorities and people who may not welcome the additional work she brings in. By sharing your time and personal attention, you show your salesperson that what she is doing is important.

2—Clear goals and expectations. Selling is a performance-based career. Those who do well get to keep doing it. Those who perform poorly do not last. But those who think they're performing well, only to learn they aren't, cannot succeed. It's like shooting an arrow at a target while blindfolded. Set clear goals and expectations, share them with the salesperson, tell her how he's doing and hold her accountable for reaching them.

3—A clean, quiet, decent place to work and the tools to do the job. Your salesperson needs a quiet place to make phone calls. She needs a desk, a chair, a phone, a place to keep files and sales tools. She needs a laptop or tablet, phone, business cards, notepads, postcards, note cards, postage, the tools of the trade. She needs software to replace some of those hard tools. She needs some way to keep track of prospect and customer contacts, whether that is a Day-Timer, smartphone or laptop. And she needs an e-mail address and Internet access without having to go to the marketing department and beg to use their computer during lunch.

4—Confidence that you, the manager, will treat his/her promises to prospects and customers with the same commitment as if you'd made them. The number one concern of almost every salesperson, from Million Dollar Club members to rookies, is that the people along the fulfillment chain will not treat their customers' jobs and deadlines with appropriate priority. Sometimes, "If I'm not there, it won't get done" is an excuse, but I hear it often from every level, so it has to be taken seriously. Procedures and systems must assure reasonable turnarounds of estimates and jobs and you, the manager, must see that commitments are kept.

5—An opportunity to be great. I rarely speak with a new sales rep who says he wants to be a poor, or even an average, performer. When he takes the job, he wants to be great. He wants to know what it takes to be Rookie of the Year. He wants to be on the Honor Roll and join the Top Performers Club. To succeed, he needs education, training, coaching and encouragement. Provide those things to an enthusiastic, goal-oriented person and stand back! Buy him sales books, send him to training courses and seminars, pay for his networking group dues, put him in touch with other successful salespeople and cheer him on.

6—Rewards and recognition. One Million Dollar Club member told me, "I make good money, but the most important thing to me is recognition. I want to be the best and to hear the applause when I pick up my sales award at the annual meeting!" We all need to hear the applause. One top performer said that in the twenty-plus years she'd worked for a major, national company, no superior had ever told her, "Good job!" Your rep wants that. She wants a handshake, a personal note of appreciation and congratulations from you. She wants you to show the whole staff that she made the Honor Roll. She wants to be introduced as your top producer. Remember the Greatest Management Principle in the World: What gets rewarded gets done.

That's what every salesperson wants.

Now, here are some suggestions for what you might give as a tangible gift:

- A book or CD by one of the sales masters: Zig Ziglar, Tom Hopkins, Brian Tracy, Harvey Mackay or Dale Carnegie.
- A certificate to attend an upcoming sales training course in your town.
- A new organizational tool
- A gift certificate for a personal item such as clothing, massage, etc.
- An item related to a personal interest like cooking, sports or home improvement.
- Something the family can share, such as a sled, a family photograph or tickets to an amusement park.

Your salesperson wants to win. You want him/her to win. The challenge is to find ways to work together, day to day, to make that happen.

What to Do Now

Need business *NOW*? Now is the time to pull out the
stops, capture new customers and position yourself for
accelerated growth. It is time to try what you have not
tried and to repeat what has been successful in securing
new business. Companies without an employed
salesperson should take the following actions this week
to try to generate immediate results. If you have a
salesperson, or more than one, the owner and
salesperson(s) each should do these things. What to do
now:

- **Call the highest-level buyers at your top 20
  accounts and set up a 20-minute meeting for a
  "market and industry interview."** In that meeting,
  ask what's going on in the company and in its
  industry. Are they growing, hiring, expanding and
  introducing new products or are they still pulling
  back, delaying new product releases and just trying
  to protect what they have? Ask what projects they
  have on the board now and what you can do to help
  make them happen.

- **Ask for business referrals.** Confirm the value of
  your business relationship, and ask for the names of
  two or three people they know who would also
  value that kind of relationship with their provider.
  Prompt them, if necessary, by asking about people
  inside the company, in their building, association,
  church, civic group, etc. Prospects to whom you are
  referred are 80% more likely to buy from you than

are cold prospects. Make this work to your advantage—this week.

- Print out the sales report that lists customers by date of last invoice and call on those who bought from you last quarter but have not ordered in 90 days. Ask what's going on in their business and what you can do for them right now. You'll be surprised at the number of them who are just waiting for you to ask.

- **Go through the quote file and call everyone who requested a quote from you in the last three months.** Whether you got the job or not, call and ask them about the job. If you did not get the job, ask what happened to it. Did it get put on hold or was it sent somewhere else? If it is on hold, is it closer to coming about? If so, can you do it for them? If it was sent somewhere else, ask why. If price was the issue, ask how much. Were they pleased with what they got? Did they get the results they needed? Will they give you a shot at their next job? If you did get the initial quote, make this a satisfaction call and ask— again—what you can do for them right now.

- **Deputize every member of your staff to sell.** Give each one 25 business cards, brochures or catalogs to distribute this week to likely prospects they see at lunch, at a restaurant, at a sporting event, at the day-care center or anywhere they spend money. Have staff members write their names on the back of the cards if they don't have their own. Offer a 10% commission on the first job over $250 that comes in from one of their business cards. If you get one minimum order from the efforts of each of your five employees, that's $1,250 in unexpected business for which you'll pay out $125. If you create a new customer, the return can be exceptional.

You need to have everybody selling, right now. This week. Go sell something.

And Finally.....

If It Is To Be...

    "Lose 10 pounds in 10 days, without diet or exercise!"
    "Get out of debt fast and cut your bills by 60%!"
    "You have inherited $260,000 (US). Forward bank information at once!"

Sure, many people fall victim to these often outrageous advertising claims. But not you. You're too smart for that. You've been around the block a time or two. You didn't just fall off the turnip truck. You know there's no such thing as a free lunch.

You're smart, tough and resourceful. That's how you survived the greatest financial crisis since The Great Depression.

You know that what works is usually the hard way, with planning and discipline and sacrifice, maybe some pain and suffering. The only way to make things work right is to get under the hood, find out what's not working and why, and then fix it up so it will work.

Except when it comes to managing salespeople. There just has to be an easy way – a book, a course, a webinar, an 800-number, a consultant, that tells you how to do it in 10 minutes, without diet or exercise? Can't you just cut a check and install some software and let someone else do it?

You know the answer in 10 words: If it is to be, it is up to me.

It is up to you...

    ...to hire right. Don't hire a sales dud. Find a rep to fit your needs, who has the mental ability to learn; the attitude, interest and motivation to perform; who has problem-solving, planning/organizing and interpersonal skills.

    ...to ensure that your salesperson is properly trained in basic selling skills and in solution selling; in your industry, product and services. Sending a new hire out to "sell" without providing him with training to do the job is akin to sending a recruit into war without the benefit of boot camp. Expect him to come back shell-shocked, bruised and bloodied, full of holes and not excited about going back out for more.

    ...to lead the sales effort. You set the direction and the focus. You set expectations and decide on how to attain them. You set the tone for the sales effort. Your attitudes, actions and communication contribute to the way your salesperson performs. You don't get to decide whether to be the leader, only whether you'll be an effective or an ineffective leader.

    ...to evaluate the performance of your salesperson(s). Management is ensuring that people do the right things, right. You and your seller must know what you want and what you don't want. And you both must know what he/she is doing and what you're getting, as a result. What gets measured gets done.

... to help them get better at doing what they must do to be successful at their job. Help them identify their strengths, skills and abilities and to improve on them. Provide the resources – books, videos, seminars, selling tools – and support that enable them to be more effective. That benefits the salesperson and you.

...to inspire your salesperson(s), which creates motivation. What motivates a person? Fear of loss or promise of gain? Money or recognition, or both? Cash or time off? All of the above. The way to know is to ask what's important to your people, and provide the incentive to perform.

Leading a successful sales team is not easy. Reading a book won't do it. Attending a seminar won't do it. Installing a software program won't do it.

If it is to be, it is up to you.

I wish you well.

www.ingramcontent.com/pod-product-compliance
Lightning Source LLC
Chambersburg PA
CBHW071844200326
41519CB00016B/4228